Copyright page

Title: Black Boy Joy and other emotions; A social - emotional learning guide and journal

Cover Design: Dr. Lisa Walker, PsyD
Editing: Lauren-Nicole
ISBN: 9798987158500

Definitions retrieved from *Merriam-Webster.com Dictionary*, Merriam-Webster, https://www.merriam-webster.com/dictionary/____. Accessed 7 Aug. 2022.

Published by QuiltedRose.org, a division of Quilted Rose Clinical Services, PLLC
Publisher's Note: This book contains general information about increasing emotional intelligence via vocabulary, journaling, coloring and related matters. The information is not medical advice. This book is not an alternative to medical advice from your doctor or other professional healthcare provider.
Our books represent the experiences and opinions of the author(s) only. Every effort has been made to ensure that events, institutions and data presented in our books as facts are accurate and up-to-date.

Names: Dr. Lisa Walker, PsyD, author.
Author's Note: This book is for informational purposes only. It is not intended as a substitute for psychotherapy from a qualified counselor. If you feel you can benefit from therapy, please consult a trained mental health professional.

For special orders, rights and permissions, please contact:

Dr. Lisa Walker, PsyD
2200 Hunt St., Ste 415, Detroit, MI 48207
info@quiltedrose.org

Printed in the United Stated of America

First edition

Black Boy Joy and other emotions
A social - emotional learning guide and journal

Hi! How are you?

This book is for young people like you to help you

- better understand deeper emotions
- how to manage your emotions
- approach and respond to others; friends, family, teachers...

*Parents are also welcomed to buy their own copy of this book to better understand how to communicate with one another and their kids. This book is the first of its kind. And we all can benefit from better emotional intelligence.

Emotions: emotions are reactions that human beings experience in response to events or situations. The type of emotions a person experiences is determined by the circumstances that trigger the emotions. All definitions in this book were retrieved from Merriam Webster™. All explanations and examples of the emotion words are the writer's own or appropriately cited.

This guide goes far beyond angry, afraid, joy, love, sadness and surprise...

Included in this workbook are

- words that might be new to you
- prompts on each page to apply the words to real life
- journal pages for you to write whatever you are thinking about
- spaces for reflection
- coping skills
- activity pages (word searches, word jumbles, coloring sheets...) so you can take a break because taking a break is important.

I truly hope you learn something about yourself and the world around you while you work through this book.

Enjoy! 😊

What do you think each of these characters are feeling?

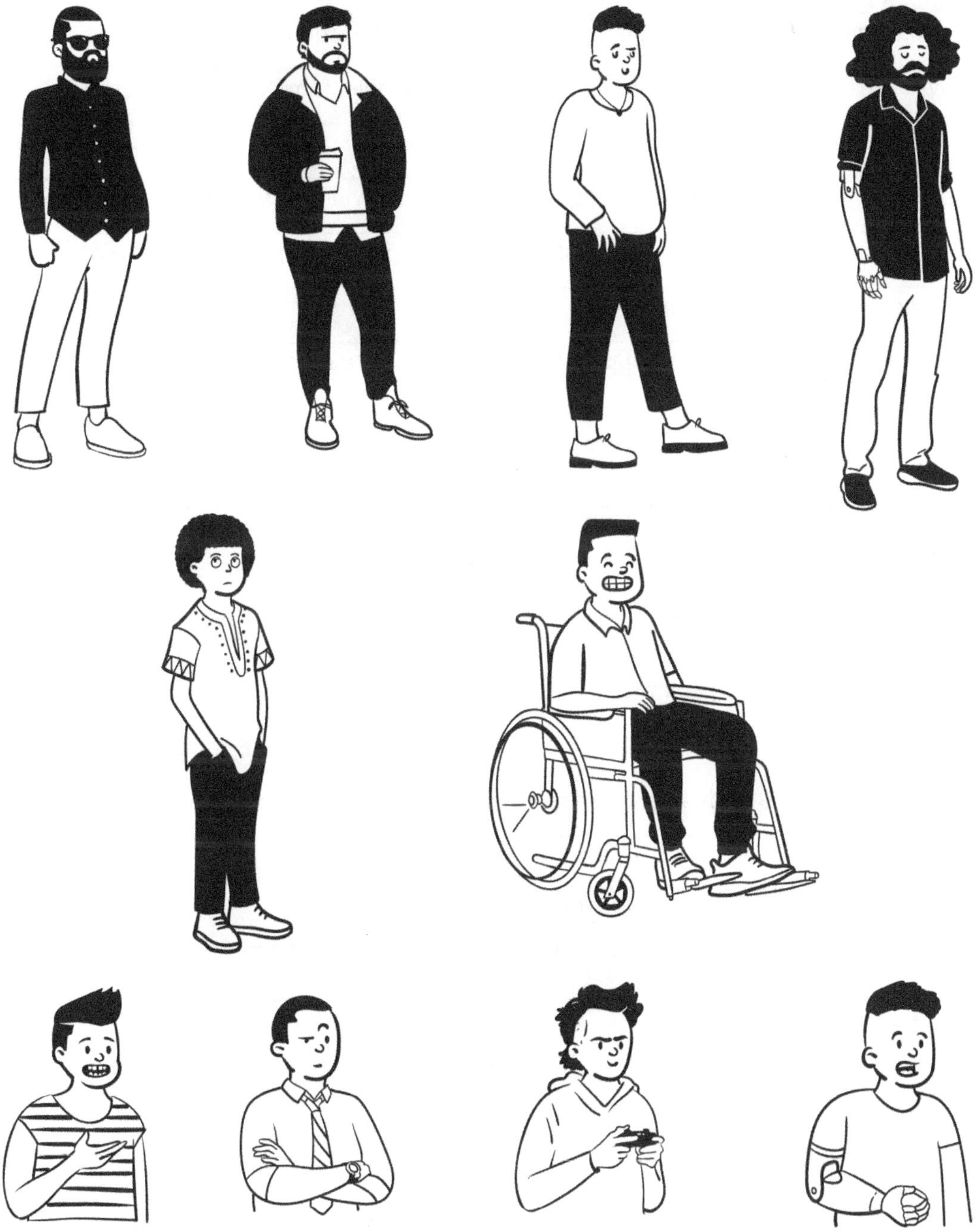

Why 3 separate books?

Each of us has unique perspectives on how we express our emotions. Some say those perspectives are most different in people who identify as male, female and people who identify as gender diverse.

This Black **Boy** Joy and other emotions... guide, and journal will help walk you through the process of helping you best define, understand and express your emotions while using he / him pronouns in the examples.

As Black boys or young men you have probably heard opposite messages about how to express yourself. Like, "Man up," "You're always angry, irritated...," "Nothing ever bothers you," "Boys / young men don't cry," "I never know how you're feeling," "Get over it," "Black boys / men don't go to therapy," "Why are you scared," "Everyone thinks you're a criminal." "Figure it out on your own," "Ask for help, you can't do it all."

It can all be very confusing, what to believe, who to listen to, all while trying to figure out who you are and who you want to be.

All of these can be true and none of them can be true. No matter what, you are human with human emotions that are to be heard and respected. It's up to you to decide who you want to be and how you want to present yourself to the world.

Be kind and don't let anyone dim your light.

DATE:

What's going on?

Free write whatever you want, however you feel

How to use this book:

Acknowledge

First, let's just acknowledge that there is a lot of information in this book.

Browse

I recommend, before diving in, that you flip through this book page-by-page.

Look at the social emotional exercises, the coping skills, the vocabulary words, the coloring sheets, everything; and then decide where you want to start.

Plan

Then make a plan; do you want to do all of the coloring sheets first? Learn all of the vocabulary words first? Learn all of the coping skills first so you can practice them over time? It's your book you have complete control.

Begin

There is no right or wrong way to work through this book. However, I would suggest that you work on one the various exercises or skills and journal in the book a little each day.

Take breaks

If you feel overwhelmed or stuck, then work on one of the coloring sheets or do a word search to refocus your thoughts and feelings.

Take your time

Learning social and emotional skills is like learning anything new; it can be challenging, it will take time and practice but it will be worth it. Especially when you notice how much you have grown and matured.

Don't forget to ask for help if you need it.

A WORD ABOUT SOCIAL INTELLIGENCE

6 BASIC EMOTIONS

Some people believe that there are [1]6 basic emotions: anger, fear, joy, love, sadness, and surprise.

Each emotion word in this book is categorized with a symbol identifying which basic emotion they are connected to. This is to help you better understand the basic meaning of the words.

But it is not meant to say that any emotion is better than any other emotion.

● anger

■ fear

▲ joy

✹ love

✦ sadness

◆ surprise

[1] Shaver P, Schwartz J, Kirson D, O'Connor C. Emotion knowledge: further exploration of a prototype approach. J Pers Soc Psychol. 1987 Jun;52(6):1061-86. doi: 10.1037//0022-3514.52.6.1061. PMID: 3598857.

CONSENT

Ask before you speak

Before you begin talking about your emotions with someone it is important to get their permission (**consent**). Getting the listener's (the person you are talking to) consent helps them prepare for what you are going to say and what they are about to hear. Also, getting consent gives the listener the chance to decline (say no or not right now). All of this is important because you want the listener to be emotionally ready to hear what you are trying to say. If the listener is not ready, you, as the talker, should respect their 'no' answer and find another way to express your emotions (example: tell someone else or journal).

Examples of how to ask for consent:

I would like to talk to you. Is that ok?

Is it ok if I tell you something?

Something happened [to me] that I would like to talk to you about?

Do you mind if I tell you how I feel about that?

If the listener says 'no', it's ok. Ask if there is a better time to talk. If not, do not pressure someone to listen to you.

Also, the person you are talking to has the right to revoke or stop consent while you are talking. Example: "I'm so sorry. I thought I was ready to listen (or be here for you) but I can't right now. Is it ok if we talk about this some other time?"

- Have you ever gotten consent from someone before talking about your emotions? How did it go?

DATE:

What's going on?

Free write whatever you want, however you feel

Take in a slow deep breath, then exhale just as slowly. How do you feel?
Pick specific colors for this coloring sheet. Which colors did you select? Why?

Mindfulness Coloring

Expressing Feelings

Feelings are not facts, but feelings (your feelings and the feelings of others) are to be heard and respected.

Feelings are best **expressed** in statements. "I feel…" statements connect the <u>emotion</u> you feel to a <u>specific issue or event</u> then provides a <u>solution</u>.

"I feel" statement formula = emotion + issue / event + solution

"I feel…" statements communicate your emotional needs while not blaming someone for "making you feel" that emotion.

- When was the last time you used an "I feel…" statement? How did it go?

DATE:

What's going on?

Free write whatever you want, however you feel

Expressing feelings using "I feel…" statements

Example: I feel appreciated when we talk without either of us looking at our phones, I hope we can do this more often.

- When was the last time you used an "I feel…" statement? How did it go?

A WORD ABOUT COPING SKILLS

*note; coping skills are spread throughout the workbook. Not just in one section.

BREATH

LIFE

TAKE IN A SLOW DEEP BREATH

EXHALE SLOWLY

UNCLENCH YOU JAW

LOWER YOUR SHOULDERS FROM YOUR EARS

Expressing feelings using "I feel..." statements

Example: I felt disappointed when you didn't call yesterday when you said you would. The next time you can't call, will you txt or send me a dm so I'm not waiting?

- When was the last time you used an "I feel..." statement? How did it go?

Expressing feelings using "I feel…" statements

Example: I feel alienated and excluded when my friends hang out without me. I would still like to be asked, even if I can't go.

- When was the last time you used an "I feel…" statement? How did it go?

Expressing feelings using "I feel..." statements

Example: I feel confident when I study for a quiz. I plan to keep working hard so I keep up my good GPA.

- When was the last time you used an "I feel..." statement? How did it go?

Expressing feelings using "I feel…" statements

Example: I felt absolutely delighted and full of glee when my father brought my baby sister with him when he picked me up from school. I hope he can bring her again.

- When was the last time you used an "I feel…" statement? How did it go?

Expressing feelings using "I feel…" statements

Example: I felt completely discombobulated, and maybe a little scared, when I first started learning how to drive and I had to merge onto the freeway, but I kept practicing and got much better quickly.

- When was the last time you used an "I feel…" statement? How did it go?

Expressing feelings using "I feel…" statements

Example: Even though my life seems ok on the outside, I can't shake this feeling of ennui and dread; I'm going to talk to my therapist about it. I really hope we can figure out what's going on.

- When was the last time you used an "I feel…" statement? How did it go?

Expressing Feelings using "I feel…" statements

Example: I feel dysregulated and out of control when my schedule changes at the last minute. I would really like if my coaches told us a week or a few days before what we are supposed to be doing.

- When was the last time you used an "I feel…" statement? How did it go?

GOSSIP

Expressing Feelings

A word about gossip.

Gossip: talk or rumors involving the personal lives of other people. “Spilling tea”

Telling gossip or listening to gossip is not a healthy way to express emotions. Gossip is harmful to the person being talked about even if they never know they are being talked about. If someone gossips to you about someone else, tell them (using **I feel statements**) that you feel uncomfortable gossiping and that you do not want to talk about this.

Example of gossip: Did you hear Jazz got kicked out of school last week? I heard they punched someone.

Appropriate response: I don’t feel comfortable talking about this. I don’t like gossip and Jazz wouldn’t appreciate us talking about them.

- How do you feel about gossip?

DATE:

What's going on?

Free write whatever you want, however you feel

Take a break and stretch

LISTENING

Consent works both ways...

When you are the **listener** (when someone is talking to you), it is important to check in with yourself to make sure you are ready to hear what they have to say. Example: If you are already upset, if you're distracted, or if you can't give the listener your full attention... it's ok to decline and get back to them as soon as possible.

Example: Now is not the best time for me to listen. Can I call you back in a couple of hours?

You should not feel or be pressured to hear someone tell you about their emotions.

Also, *you have the right to stop consent while the other person is talking to you about strong emotions.*

Example: "I'm so sorry. I thought I was ready to listen (or be here for you) but I'm not emotionally ready to hear this right now. Is it ok if we talk about this later when I get home and I can give you my full attention?"

- Was there ever a time when someone was sharing something personal with you and you stopped consent? Was there a time when someone was talking to you, and you wished you had stopped consent? What happened?

DATE:

What's going on?

Free write whatever you want, however you feel

HARM AND CONSENT

Harm and consent... (non-abusive)

If someone has harmed you - YOU can choose if you want to ask for their consent to talk to them about what happened.

When expressing your feelings, it's good to remember to use "I feel..." statements:

Emotion + issue / event + solution

If someone tries to joke about the harm they have caused you it is ok to say to them "that's not funny" and walk away. Only allow the person to reenter your space when they have addressed the issue and, at least tried to correct the harm they caused.

Example: I felt embarrassed when you spread rumors about me being kicked out of school. I would appreciate it if you never did that again and if you have questions about where I have been, please ask me.

Have you ever told someone that they harmed you? What happened?

DATE:

What's going on?

Free write whatever you want, however you feel

Take a slow deep breath, then exhale just as slowly. How do you feel?
Pick specific colors for this coloring sheet. Which colors did you select. Why?

Mindfulness Coloring

SAFETY

Safety is like the concepts of consent and boundaries

Feeling emotionally safe and being physically safe are very different.

Being physically safe is like wearing a seat belt in a car.

While emotional safety involves being in a space (home, school, park...) or with specific people and you physically notice that your body is relaxed, the people present have consistently shown to respect your boundaries, where it's ok to speak up and be heard, where it's ok to make mistakes, where being challenged comes from a place of compassion versus being punitive and where individualism (being yourself within community) is celebrated.

- Describe where you feel most safe

DATE:

What's going on?

Free write whatever you want, however you feel

SELF AWARENESS

Self-awareness is the ability to have knowledge of your character, feelings, motives (Why am I doing this?) and desires.

Being self-aware is necessary because if you are not self-aware you cannot understand the impact you have on other people (good or bad).

In addition to impact, self-awareness has several other benefits; being self-aware helps you make better decisions, it helps you know what you want and do not want, you can accept feedback, criticism, and compliments constructively, and self-awareness helps you see things from other people's perspective.

Self-awareness is very different from being *self-conscious*. Being self-conscious is essentially feeling or being uncomfortable about being looked at (or heard) by others. Being self-conscious focuses on negative traits or behaviors with no recognition of your positive qualities.

- People usually become more self-aware as they get older. How have you noticed your awareness of yourself change?

DATE:

What's going on?

Free write whatever you want, however you feel

A BRIEF WORD ABOUT ABUSE

Harm and consent... (ABUSIVE)

If someone has harmed you sexually (touch or words), physically (hit, kicked, bit...) or emotionally (threatened you, threatened someone you know, put you down...) **do not talk to the person directly**.

Tell a safe adult what happened. Tell the adult the facts (when, where, what...) and how you felt. You should feel like the adult you tell understands and believes you. The adult you tell should then make sure you are safe and take care of the situation. If you do not feel seen and heard, tell another adult. Keep telling as many adults as possible until you are safe.

Example of dangerous harm: Yesterday in science class my lab partner showed me a knife. They said that if I didn't do the entire project myself they would cut me and my friends when we weren't looking.

Example of an appropriate response: I'm so sorry that happened to you. I will make sure that student does not harm you or your friends. *The bully is removed from the school, the parents of all children are told. The police may be called as well, an adult checks on you to make sure you feel safe. *

Have you ever told someone that you were harmed? What happened?

DATE:

What's going on?

Free write whatever you want, however you feel

Harm and consent...

If you have harmed someone you may not have the choice as to when you can hear someone express their emotions to you.

If you have harmed someone, it is important that you,

- listen respectfully
- tell the person you harmed that you understand what you did was not ok
- sincerely apologize
- do what you can to correct the mistake

Causing harm to someone is not a joke or funny.

Example of how to apologize when you have caused harm to someone: I understand you are upset. I should not have been playing around with your phone. Now your screen is cracked. I can send you the money to have it fixed, is that ok?

Has someone ever told you that you harmed them? What happened?

More LISTENING

Listening to others express themselves is just as important as **learning** about feeling words and **expressing** feelings.

Listening works best when you give the person speaking your full attention (put your phone down and try not to interrupt).

When was the last time you listened to someone express their emotions to you and you gave them your full attention? How did it go? What happened?

DATE:

What's going on?

Free write whatever you want, however you feel

Listening

If you do not understand what someone is saying it's ok to ask them to repeat what they said or ask them to say it in a different way using different words.

Example: I'm sorry I don't understand what you mean by...? What does [insert word] mean?

Have you ever had to ask someone to clarify something they were telling you? How did it go? What happened?

Listening

Being a good listener also means *actually* hearing (to learn) the words the person is saying and responding to what **they** are saying. Not listening just for your turn to talk.

Example (after a friend stops speaking): I'm so sorry that happened to you. How can I help?

When was the last time you listened to someone express their emotions to you?

How did it go?

Take a break and listen to music

Listening	
Another important part of being a good listener is using language of compassion and understanding. Using language of compassion and understanding means not blaming and not automatically assuming the person talking to you is wrong.	
Instead of:	Maybe say:
What's wrong with you?	What happened? What's going on?
Why did you do that?	Let's think about some ways that may give you a better outcome / response?
Why did you say that?	Is there another way that could have been said to maybe get you a better outcome / response?
Stop crying / don't cry Why are you being so dramatic?	It's ok to cry. How can I help? What's going on?
Just get over it / Move on...	I'm so sorry that happened to you
Everything is going to be ok	I'm so sorry that happened to you I'm so sorry you're going through this How can I support / help you?
When was the last time you listened to someone express their emotions to you?	
How did it go?	

Listening

Sometimes when someone is telling you personal information, they take pauses to get their words together.

Silence is ok.

You don't need to say anything to be a good listener.

Are you comfortable with sitting with someone who is emotional but not saying anything?

Have you ever done this? How did you feel sitting in silence?

Listening

Sometimes when someone is telling you personal information, they just want someone to talk to, **or** they want your opinion or advice. It's important to give them the option.

Example: "Would you like for me to just listen, or would you like some feedback (or advice)?"

Are you comfortable listening without giving advice? Have you ever tried it? How did it go?

Listening

Usually when someone tells you personal information, they do not want that information shared with other people without their permission. It's best to just not tell anyone - someone else's business, even if it has been a long time since they told you.

But there are times when someone tells you private information and you may be afraid that the person is in danger or that they may harm someone. When that happens, if you feel safe, tell the person sharing information with you, that you are not comfortable keeping this information private and tell a safe adult.

Remember to state the facts and to keep telling adults until you are heard and believed.

SENSATIONS

Have you ever noticed how your body feels when you're in certain places or with certain people?

If you typically feel anxious, nervous, upset… when you're with someone, talk (using "I feel…" statements) about how you feel.

Example when speaking with you therapist: Every time I hang out with Que my stomach feels like it's in knots and I don't know why.

Also, when you are with someone and you usually feel good, it's ok to tell them.

Example: I really like hanging out with you. We can have fun and talk about serious stuff too.

DATE:

What's going on?

Free write whatever you want, however you feel

Take in a slow deep breath, then exhale just as slowly. How do you feel?
Pick specific colors for this coloring sheet. Which colors did you select? Why?

Mindfulness Coloring

DID YOU MOVE YOUR BODY TODAY

BOUNDARIES

It cannot be stressed enough how important boundaries are in emotional intelligence.

Boundaries are like consent. Remember, you always have the right to say "**NO**."

There are multiple types of boundaries:

• Physical	• Sexual
• Emotional or mental	• Spiritual or religious
• Financial and material	• Time

You have the right to express your boundaries and respecting the boundaries of others is equally as important.

Are there other types of boundaries you can think of?

Are you comfortable setting and keeping your boundaries?

DATE:

What's going on?

Free write whatever you want, however you feel

HOW TO SET HEALTHY BOUNDARIES

Boundaries are important for your mental wellbeing as they establish personal limits between you and anyone you interact with.

Here's how you can start

1. Identify Your Needs & Values

What makes you happy/sad/angry and what can you not tolerate?

2. Express How You Feel

Let people know how you feel and set ground rules.

3. The Art of Saying No

The word 'no' is a complete statement.

*Setting boundaries is not easy and probably won't feel very good. But that is kind of the point. As you grow and mature you will become more secure in your values making setting boundaries easier.

Also, boundaries are not the same as holding a grudge.

Reminder of the emotion words categories from page 7:

● anger ■ fear ▲ joy ☀ love ✦ sadness ◆ surprise

A WORD ABOUT INCREASING EMOTIONAL LITERACY

Emotion vocabulary word: adoration

Meaning: deep love and respect

Example: "I find fame to be quite unnatural. Humans are not built for extreme adoration." - Jada Pinkett Smith

Have you heard this word before? Y / N

Now that you know this feeling word, are there other words that you can think of that have a similar meaning?

Have you ever felt adoration? Y / N

What was going on?

It's ok to reach out when things are going well and when they are not.

Did you check on someone today? Y / N

How did it go?

DATE:

What's going on?

Free write whatever you want, however you feel

Emotion vocabulary word: alienation

Meaning: the act of turning away, transferring, or diverting

Example: I feel alienated and excluded when my friends hang out without me. I would still like to be asked, even if I can't go.

Have you heard this word before? Y / N

Now that you know this feeling word, are there other words that you can think of that have a similar meaning?

Have you ever felt alienation? Y / N

What was going on?

It's ok to reach out when things are going well and when they are not.

Did you check on someone today? Y / N

How did it go?

DATE:

What's going on?

Free write whatever you want, however you feel

Emotion vocabulary word: aversion

Meaning: a person or thing that arouses strong feelings of dislike.

Example: They had a deep-seated aversion to unseasoned food.

Have you heard this word before? Y / N

Now that you know this feeling word, are there other words that you can think of that have a similar meaning?

Have you ever experienced aversion? Y / N

What was going on?

It's ok to reach out when things are going well and when they are not.

Did you check on someone today? Y / N

How did it go?

DATE:

What's going on?

Free write whatever you want, however you feel

word search

DO YOU EVER STRUGGLE TO FIND YOUR WORDS?
WELL LOOK FOR THEM HERE!

A B O A P O M X C F I X J K W S W H R J W R A

U G Q F M Z H A G I T A T I O N E K Q F Y S N

R H K G L G N O Y T M A S T O N I S H E D S N

U I V X A F R A I D F S K A M N B X P A S P O

A Y I A E A B E R Y A L A R M E D H P D P C Y

V B E A N T I C I P A T I N G A A W Q M Z R E

Y U N B O J R M P P G B X Z S N A K M I Z T D

A J E S L P D X J Y N I B P N G C O I R R B L

S D A P P R E H E N S I O N Q E D B R A C Q R

S J B A A S A A G U A G I H F R N B D T A Q A

E N A R M F W P I L Y R A L I E N A T I O N D

R H V R A I E A Q C V L Z A L A R M Z O R W Y

T H E O Z I S T A L A T T E N T I V E N E S S

I T R G E J L H D N B V R N M G M L U G A A W

V X S A M R Z Y O A C C E P T A N C E J T F X

E W I N E I U O R A M B I V A L E N C E T F R

E K O T N J J K A A G G R E S S I V E T R E S

W Q N P T I E Y T N U A M U S E M E N T A C O

A A N X I O U S I G A X W D S Z V Y A P C T R

F H K I J E C S O U P W E G T S U D G K T I J

Q E E N F M A X N I O C V V J F F S O M I O O

B U I M H T A D N S X S Z V Y N X O N L O N O

Y F R T K R Z B I H W H F L K U U Q Y Z N U V

1

AGGRESSIVE, ALIENATION, ATTRACTION, APATHY, ACCEPTANCE,
ALARMED, ANGUISH, ADORATION, ANXIOUS, ANGER, APPREHENSION,
ASTONISHED, AFFECTION, AVERSION, ANTICIPATING, ATTENTIVENESS,
AMAZEMENT, ARROGANT, AFRAID, ADMIRATION, AMUSEMENT, AWE,
ALARM, AMBIVALENCE, ASSERTIVE, AGONY, AGITATION, ANNOYED

Emotion vocabulary word: bliss

Meaning: perfect happiness; great joy

Example: He gave a sigh of pure bliss after getting His hair done.

Have you heard this word before? Y / N

Now that you know this feeling word, are there other words that you can think of that have a similar meaning?

Have you ever experienced bliss? Y / N

What was going on?

It's ok to reach out when things are going well and when they are not.

Did you check on someone today? Y / N

How did it go?

DATE:

What's going on?

Free write whatever you want, however you feel

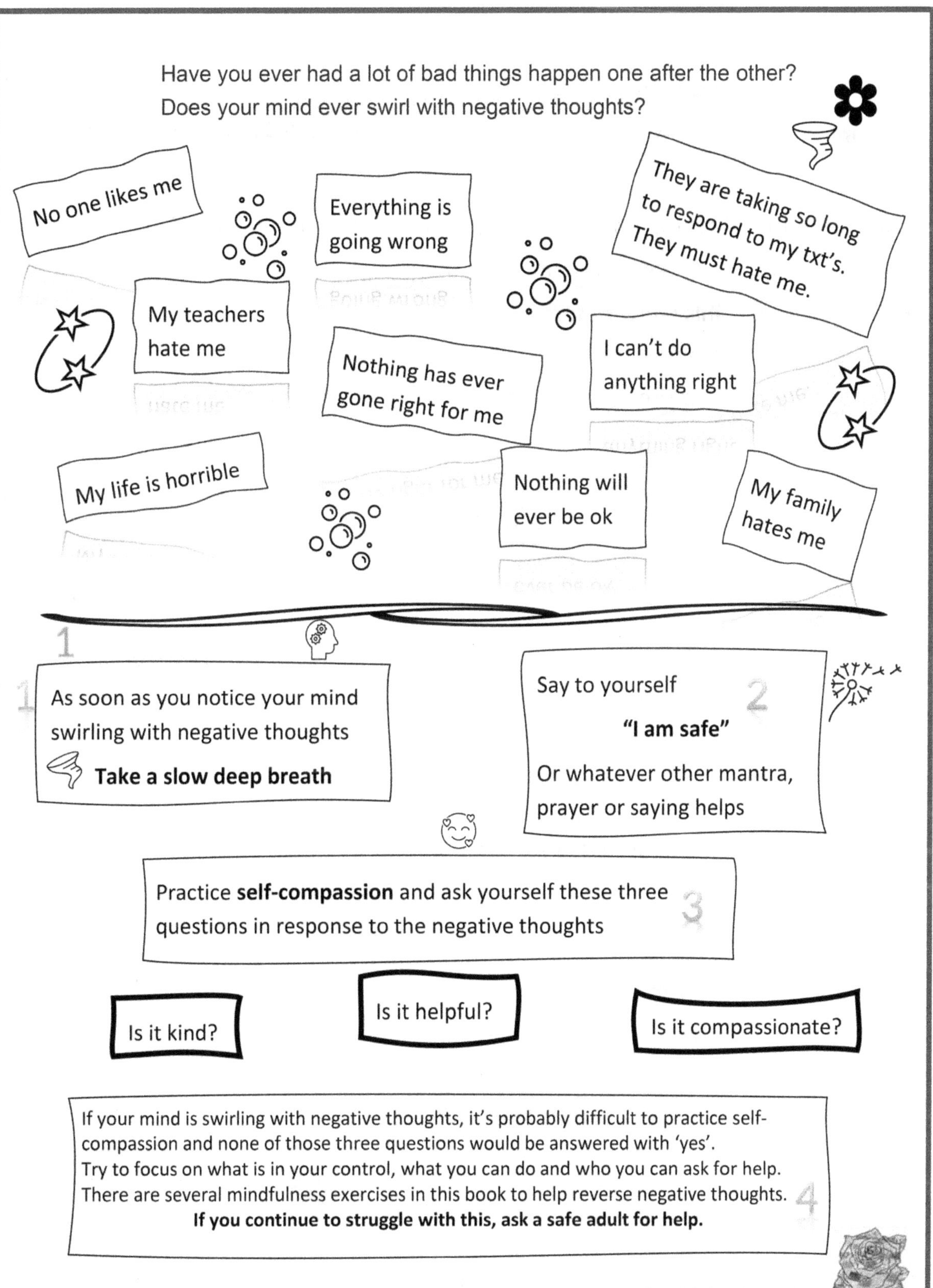
Have you ever had a lot of bad things happen one after the other?
Does your mind ever swirl with negative thoughts?
No one likes me
Everything is going wrong
They are taking so long to respond to my txt's. They must hate me.
My teachers hate me
Nothing has ever gone right for me
I can't do anything right
My life is horrible
Nothing will ever be ok
My family hates me
1
As soon as you notice your mind swirling with negative thoughts
Take a slow deep breath
Say to yourself
"I am safe"
Or whatever other mantra, prayer or saying helps
2
Practice self-compassion and ask yourself these three questions in response to the negative thoughts
3
Is it kind?
Is it helpful?
Is it compassionate?
If your mind is swirling with negative thoughts, it's probably difficult to practice self-compassion and none of those three questions would be answered with 'yes'.
Try to focus on what is in your control, what you can do and who you can ask for help.
There are several mindfulness exercises in this book to help reverse negative thoughts.
If you continue to struggle with this, ask a safe adult for help.
4

Emotion vocabulary word: brazen

Meaning: bold and without shame; brazen means the opposite of shy.

Example: He went about his illegal business with a brazen attitude like he would never be caught.

Have you heard this word before? Y / N

Now that you know this feeling word, are there other words that you can think of that have a similar meaning?

Have you ever felt or acted brazen? Y / N

What was going on?

It's ok to reach out when things are going well and when they are not.

Did you check on someone today? Y / N

How did it go?

DATE:

What's going on?

Free write whatever you want, however you feel

Emotion vocabulary word: cheeky

Meaning: impudent or irreverent, typically in an endearing or amusing way.

Example: He gave a cheeky grin to the cashier when he was given some of the items for free.

Have you heard this word before? Y / N

Now that you know this feeling word, are there other words that you can think of that have a similar meaning?

Have you ever felt cheeky? Y / N

What was going on?

It's ok to reach out when things are going well and when they are not.

Did you check on someone today? Y / N

How did it go?

DATE:

What's going on?

Free write whatever you want, however you feel

Emotion vocabulary word: compassion

Meaning: an understanding of another's pain and the desire to somehow mitigate that pain.

Compassion is a step beyond empathy because with compassion someone tries to lessen the pain the hurt person is feeling.

Example: Mr. Wada showed compassion by giving extra time for the homework to be due after I was sick.

Have you heard this word before? Y / N

Now that you know this feeling word, are there other words that you can think of that have a similar meaning?

Have you ever experienced compassion? Y / N

What was going on?

It's ok to reach out when things are going well and when they are not.

Did you check on someone today? Y / N

How did it go?

DATE:

What's going on?

Free write whatever you want, however you feel

DO YOU EVER STRUGGLE TO FIND YOUR WORDS?
WELL FIND THEM HERE!!

word searc

```
D P Z N W Y M A D E T E R M I N E D J Q T X
I O W U S B D X D I S P L E A S U R E D W U
S D I S O R I E N T E D A D D U O S C I C Z
P R G D D I S G U S T I D I E A O U G S X U
I E X U A D C A A W D S I S M Z D S D G A E
R A J D K I O M D E U C S C O V D Y I R T D
I D D I B S M U G V M O H O R A C S S U H J
T L Z S G M F J X M B M E N A S A D B N D I
E I C T U A O A V Q S B A T L B U E E T R S
D L Y R Z Y R J N Q T O R E I N K J L L I B
W B F E A S T I T L R B T N Z F D E I E V W
O D I S T U R B E D U U E T E J I C E D E N
W D I S L I K E O Z C L N M D A S T F B N D
D E P R E S S E D Q K A E E P H T I K V K E
Z G C H K K O D T Q B T D N A E R O A B H S
O N M C A W I A Z D L E K T L D A N S W R P
A R B W S B D Z Q G H D J N Z O C R I E D A
D E L I G H T E D W R X E H K U T L V Y I I
U B V S M T N D P B H J S F H B I L J S G R
C I D I S A P P O I N T M E N T O H R R U L
N D E S I R E F G B U A B Z D F N Z E U V R
K C M D D O M I N A N T I P S N H U C E L E
```

2

DREAD, DISTRESS, DISCOMBOBULATED,

DEMORALIZED, DESIRE, DOMINANT, DISBELIEF,

DETERMINED, DISGUST, DRIVEN, DESPAIR,

DISTRACTION, DISLIKE, DISCONTENTMENT,

DISAPPOINTMENT, DUMBSTRUCK, DAZED,

DEPRESSED, DISPIRITED, DOUBT, DISPLEASURE,

DISORIENTED, DISTURBED, DISMAY, DELIGHTED,

DISHEARTENED, DEJECTION, DISCOMFORT,

DISGRUNTLED

take a break and stretch

Emotion vocabulary word: cynicism

Meaning: an inclination to believe that people are motivated purely by self-interest; skepticism.

Example: "Cynicism is the greatest barrier to love. It is rooted in doubt and despair. Fear intensifies our doubt. It paralyzes. Faith and hope allow us to let go. Fear stands in the way of love." - bell hooks

Have you heard this word before? Y / N

Now that you know this feeling word, are there other words that you can think of that have a similar meaning?

Have you ever experienced cynicism? Y / N

What was going on?

It's ok to reach out when things are going well and when they are not.

Did you check on someone today? Y / N

How did it go?

DATE:

What's going on?

Free write whatever you want, however you feel

Emotion vocabulary word: delighted

Meaning: feeling or showing great pleasure

Example: "We are delighted in the beauty of the butterfly, but rarely admit the changes it has gone through to achieve that beauty." – Maya Angelou

Have you heard this word before? Y / N

Now that you know this feeling word, are there other words that you can think of that have a similar meaning?

Have you ever felt delighted? Y / N

What was going on?

It's ok to reach out when things are going well and when they are not.

Did you check on someone today? Y / N

How did it go?

DATE:

What's going on?

Free write whatever you want, however you feel

Emotion vocabulary word: discombobulated

Meaning: confused and disconcerted

Example: He looked a little pained and discombobulated when the mechanic, out of nowhere, started free-style rapping.

Have you heard this word before? Y / N

Now that you know this feeling word, are there other words that you can think of that have a similar meaning?

Have you ever felt discombobulated? Y / N

What was going on?

It's ok to reach out when things are going well and when they are not.

Did you check on someone today? Y / N

How did it go?

DATE:

What's going on?

Free write whatever you want, however you feel

vitdoamet	=	____________	senadniugnrtd	=	____________	ptiy	=	____________
nepcgteirs	=	____________	osnccusoi	=	____________	lefs	=	____________
iatglhon	=	____________	lcaictri	=	____________	narcgi	=	____________

Do you ever struggle to pronounce or spell words?
Test your skills with these emotion words here!
*Hint; all of these words typically begin with the word "self".

word scramble

3

Emotion vocabulary word: elated ▲

Meaning: marked by high spirits; the opposite of depressed.

Example: He was elated to learn that he was accepted to her first- choice HBCU.

Have you heard this word before? Y / N

Now that you know this feeling word, are there other words that you can think of that have a similar meaning?

Have you ever felt or acted elated? Y / N

What was going on?

It's ok to reach out when things are going well and when they are not.

Did you check on someone today? Y / N

How did it go?

DATE:

What's going on?

Free write whatever you want, however you feel

Take in a slow deep breath, then exhale just as slowly. How do you feel?
Pick specific colors for this coloring sheets. Which colors did you select? Why?

Mindfulness Coloring

Emotion vocabulary word: ennui *(pronounced ahn-we)*

Meaning: a feeling of utter weariness and discontent resulting from satiety or lack of interest; boredom.

Example: Many teenagers dealing with the world at large may have more devices in-hand now, but unpredictable emotions and ennui persists.

Have you heard this word before? Y / N

Now that you know this feeling word, are there other words that you can think of that have a similar meaning?

Have you ever felt ennui? Y / N

What was going on?

It's ok to reach out when things are going well and when they are not.

Did you check on someone today? Y / N

How did it go?

DATE:

What's going on?

Free write whatever you want, however you feel

Emotion vocabulary word: epiphany ▲

Meaning: a moment when you suddenly feel that you understand, or suddenly become conscious of something that is very important to you.

Example: Seeing his father again as an adult was an epiphany that epiphany that changed his whole view of childhood.

Have you heard this word before? Y / N

Now that you know this feeling word, are there other words that you can think of that have a similar meaning?

Have you ever experienced an epiphany? Y / N

What was going on?

It's ok to reach out when things are going well and when they are not.

Did you check on someone today? Y / N

How did it go?

DATE:

What's going on?

Free write whatever you want, however you feel

Emotion vocabulary word: exasperated

Meaning: intensely irritated and frustrated.

Example: He felt exasperated after realizing he still had 3 more hours of school.

Have you heard this word before? Y / N

Now that you know this feeling word, are there other words that you can think of that have a similar meaning?

Have you ever felt exasperated? Y / N

What was going on?

It's ok to reach out when things are going well and when they are not.

Did you check on someone today? Y / N

How did it go?

DATE:

What's going on?

Free write whatever you want, however you feel

DO YOU EVER STRUGGLE TO FIND YOUR WORDS? WELL FIND THEM HERE!!

word search

C J Q C C Z V I C R U E L T Y N H I T J G
Y B F Z U A C L A U S T R O P H O B I C G
N I I Z V L L H M B H S P J C O N T E N T
I L R L H U S P Y A J C O N T E M P T F K
C I W P G N K J B F W H N G C O U R A G E
I B R O O D I N G F U M H V E Y S Q V J H
S Q F I A C B N N L C O M F O R T A B L E
M Z P V F V E Y N E B R A Z E N P G J Y K
C A X M I R W F Z D Y Q C O N F U S I O N
S Z O E C C I W X C A R I N G H K H C O J
X V N H H G L I C O M P A S S I O N O N K
L O N C E D D Q R R G Z A E W N K Z E R J
C S O A E C E C D D E L Y H K E C C R H B
B C V R R H R H G K M O D L C A L M C R N
N A P E F A E E Y S V F U H Y B Q S I X H
B R B L U R D E C O W A R D L Y G M V L K
A E B E L I X K J V M B C O N F I D E N T
Q F Z S N T S Y I U N O C U R I O S I T Y
Q R Y S E Y Z K G K P R D Z F P B L I S S
N E O N S N Q N F F Y E B A B I T T E R M
M E S J S F X M D O Q D H Y E K G W L X M

4

CHEEKY, CARING, BAFFLED, CRUELTY, BRAZEN,

CALM, COMFORTABLE, COWARDLY, CHARITY,

BORED, CONTENT, CHEERFULNESS, COERCIVE,

CONFIDENT, COMPASSION, CONTEMPT, CURIOSITY,

CONFUSION, BITTER, CYNICISM, BLISS, CAREFREE,

CARELESS, BEWILDERED, CLAUSTROPHOBIC,

BROODING, COURAGE

Emotion vocabulary word: fascination

Meaning: very charming, attractive or interesting; the opposite of disinterested.

Example: There is a fascination with copying Black culture in popular media, but not a fascination in crediting Black creators.

Have you heard this word this before? Y / N

Now that you know this feeling word, are there other words that you can think of that have a similar meaning?

Have you ever experienced fascination with someone or something? Y / N

What was going on?

It's ok to reach out when things are going well and when they are not.

Did you check on someone today? Y / N

How did it go?

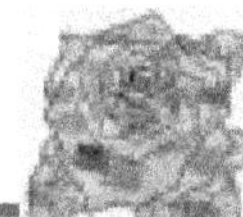

DATE:

What's going on?

Free write whatever you want, however you feel

Have you ever noticed yourself being irritated or something just not feeling right? Like something is just off? HALT can be a useful acronym to use to find out what's going on and to work through it.

Hunger: getting a snack or something to eat is pretty straight forward. Try to recognize hunger cues before you become hanrgy. And, ask yourself if you are hungry for food, thristy or hungry for emotional connection.

Anger: is a normal human emotion. Anger is just as valid of an emotion as all emotions. It is important to HALT and discover the source of your anger. What part of your body is being activated? What emotion or memory of being triggered? Can you address the situation without regretting it later?

Loneliness: can happen when you're in a room full of people who you know or if you are alone in your bedroom. If you are in a space where you don't feel seen, understood or respected this can lead to feeling lonely. Where do you feel safest? Is there someone you can reach out to?

Tiredeness: sometimes we ignore when our bodies are telling us to slow down and take a nap. Sometimes it's completely inappropiate to slow down and take a nap. But tiredness is a normal bodily function telling us that we haven't had enough restful sleep. Examine why. Did you stay up late doing homework? Do you sleep with your phone and scroll on social media or txt all night? Is your home noisy? Does your mind overthink and you can't get to sleep?

Some good strategies for restful sleep are; no phone for 3 hours before bed, journal before bed to get out any thoughts that may be keeping you awake, stretch or do some light yoga to get any restless energy out.

Emotion vocabulary word: fondness

Meaning: affection or liking for someone or something; the opposite of hatred.

Example: I have always held a fondness for '90 hip-hop and rap.

Have you heard this word this before? Y / N

Now that you know this feeling word, are there other words that you can think of that have a similar meaning?

Have you ever felt fondness? Y / N

What was going on?

It's ok to reach out when things are going well and when they are not.

Did you check on someone today? Y / N

How did it go?

DATE:

What's going on?

Free write whatever you want, however you feel

Emotion vocabulary word: gratitude

Meaning: the quality of being thankful; readiness to show appreciation for and to return kindness.

Example: I felt gratitude for the person who helped change my tire.

Have you heard this word this before? Y / N

Now that you know this feeling word, are there other words that you can think of that have a similar meaning?

Have you ever felt or expressed gratitude? Y / N

What was going on?

It's ok to reach out when things are going well and when they are not.

Did you check on someone today? Y / N

How did it go?

DATE:

What's going on?

Free write whatever you want, however you feel

Emotion vocabulary word: guilt

Meaning: the fact of having committed a specified or implied offense or crime. The opposite of guilt is innocence.

Example: Assumed innocence versus assumed guilt is a privilege.

Have you heard this word this before? Y / N

Now that you know this feeling word, are there other words that you can think of that have a similar meaning?

Have you ever felt or experienced guilt? Y / N

What was going on?

It's ok to reach out when things are going well and when they are not.

Did you check on someone today? Y / N

How did it go?

DATE:

What's going on?

Free write whatever you want, however you feel

Emotion vocabulary word: intrigue

Meaning: arouse the curiosity or interest of; to fascinate.

Intrigue means the opposite of uninterested.

Example: He expressed intrigue about the new Jordan 1's.

Have you heard this word this before? Y / N

Now that you know this feeling word, are there other words that you can think of that have a similar meaning?

Have you ever felt intrigue? Y / N

What was going on?

It's ok to reach out when things are going well and when they are not.

Did you check on someone today? Y / N

How did it go?

DATE:

What's going on?

Free write whatever you want, however you feel

This is a relaxation skill and coping tool for when you are stressed.
It works best if you practice this when you are *relaxed* (daily is preferable) so when / if you get stressed it's easy to recall.
If you do not practice this when you are relaxed it will be more difficult to remember what to do when you are stressed.
Try it now. Then try teaching a friend or family member.

TRIANGLE BREATHING

EXHALE – 4 COUNT

INHALE – 4 COUNT

HOLD – 4 COUNT

Emotion vocabulary word: jovial

Meaning: suggests cheerful, joyous, uninhibited enjoyment of frolic or festivity.

Example: Drake's latest release is so jovial that I feel like dancing every time I listen to it.

Have you heard this word this before? Y / N

Now that you know this feeling word, are there other words that you can think of that have a similar meaning?

Have you ever felt jovial? Y / N

What was going on?

It's ok to reach out when things are going well and when they are not.

Did you check on someone today? Y / N

How did it go?

DATE:

What's going on?

Free write whatever you want, however you feel

Emotion vocabulary word: loathing

Meaning: strong dislike or disgust; intense aversion.

Example: The thought of wearing one brand of sneakers and another brand's track suit filled them with loathing.

Have you heard this word before? Y / N

Now that you know this feeling word, are there other words that you can think of that have a similar meaning?

Have you ever felt loathing? Y / N

What was going on?

It's ok to reach out when things are going well and when they are not.

Did you check on someone today? Y / N

How did it go?

DATE:

What's going on?

Free write whatever you want, however you feel

Emotion vocabulary word: loopy

Meaning: befuddled or confused, especially due to intoxication.

Example: Novocain caused him to be a little loopy after having his wisdom teeth pulled.

Have you heard this word before? Y / N

Now that you know this feeling word, are there other words that you can think of that have a similar meaning?

Have you ever felt loopy? Y / N

What was going on?

It's ok to reach out when things are going well and when they are not.

Did you check on someone today? Y / N

How did it go?

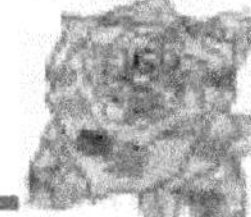

DATE:

What's going on?

Free write whatever you want, however you feel

K I N S I D I O U S I A D Q E N Z C I U A

M Z Y T N I D I O T I C G G F B G C I T H

A B S L Q H M I S E R A B L E C P E G C M

X J R D U U K N M I X E D   U P A S X S K

Q F U Z I H I L A R I O U S M H L P W F C

P A M B S Q B O M W N Q J X O V E I F H A

M S C T I H F N I M O O D Y R O P M I R G

E Y J L T H O G S A E U R L T U A H R L E

L D B M I U P I E E U N V S I V S Y S W Y

A E Z O V A L N R I S K Z Q F L U S T Q F

N M A D E B O G L M O E A U I Z W M V X V

C W Q E A S N Y I Y D V Z Q E E L N G P B

H L U S T H E I N S M F Y V D K I E B O Y

O T T T E A L Y E T V D L O O P Y B P W O

L O R Y I L Y A S I F R E L X K Z U W E R

Y H I O B T Z S S F D U N O W O J L R R Q

D M L I K I N G J I C N S V C N X O V F F

A A X V F N W N O E G K V E N U N U R U W

A L F U H G G D L D E C L O U D Y S L L W

A E S K U L A Z Y O I B I E S R N F H E V

L O A T H I N G V O X G T P U W W V O E U

DO YOU EVER STRUGGLE TO FIND YOUR WORDS?
WELL FIND THEM HERE!!

5

CAGEY, HALTING, LAZY, MORTIFIED, LONELY, IDIOTIC, LONGING, LOVE, PALE, MALE, NEBULOUS, MYSTIFIED, LOATHING, LOOPY, LUST, MELANCHOLY, INQUISITIVE, MISERLINESS, DRUNK, FIRST, HILARIOUS, MAD, POWERFUL, MISERABLE, MIXED UP, INSIDIOUS, LIKING, CLOUDY, MOODY, MODESTY

word search

Emotion vocabulary word: melancholy

Meaning: a feeling of pensive sadness, typically with no obvious cause. Melancholy means the opposite of cheerful.

Example: At first listen Kendrick Lamar's latest album sounded melancholy However, after listening to his other album's, his evolution as an artist is clear.

Have you heard this word before? Y / N

Now that you know this feeling word, are there other words that you can think of that have a similar meaning?

Have you ever felt melancholy? Y / N

What was going on?

It's ok to reach out when things are going well and when they are not.

Did you check on someone today? Y / N

How did it go?

DATE:

What's going on?

Free write whatever you want, however you feel

Emotion vocabulary word: miserliness

Meaning: of, like, or befitting a miser, penurious; stingy.

Example: Parents tend to act with miserliness when their children ask for food while out, and there is food at home.

Have you heard this word before? Y / N

Now that you know this feeling word, are there other words that you can think of that have a similar meaning?

Have you ever felt miserliness? Y / N

What was going on?

It's ok to reach out when things are going well and when they are not.

Did you check on someone today? Y / N

How did it go?

DATE:

What's going on?

Free write whatever you want, however you feel

Emotion vocabulary word: mortified

Meaning: humiliated, ashamed, or deeply embarrassed.

Example: He was mortified when his teacher called on him to answer the question, and he had not completed the assigned reading.

Have you heard this word before? Y / N

Now that you know this feeling word, are there other words that you can think of that have a similar meaning?

Have you ever been mortified? Y / N

What was going on?

It's ok to reach out when things are going well and when they are not.

Did you check on someone today? Y / N

How did it go?

DATE:

What's going on?

Free write whatever you want, however you feel

Take in a slow deep breath, then exhale just as slowly. How do you feel?
Pick specific colors for this coloring sheet. Which colors did you select? Why?

Mindfulness Coloring

practice triangle breathing

Emotion vocabulary word: nostalgic

Meaning: experiencing or exhibiting a sentimental or wistful yearning for the happiness felt in a former place, time, or situation.

Example: He is nostalgic for his childhood home after moving.

Have you heard this word before? Y / N

Now that you know this feeling word, are there other words that you can think of that have a similar meaning?

Have you ever been nostalgic? Y / N

What was going on?

It's ok to reach out when things are going well and when they are not.

Did you check on someone today? Y / N

How did it go?

DATE:

What's going on?

Free write whatever you want, however you feel

Emotion vocabulary word: obstinate

Meaning: firmly or stubbornly adhering to one's purpose, opinion, etc.; not yielding to argument, persuasion, or entreaty.

Example: He was obstinate about pursuing a career in music

Have you heard this word before? Y / N

Now that you know this feeling word, are there other words that you can think of that have a similar meaning?

Have you ever felt obstinate? Y / N

What was going on?

It's ok to reach out when things are going well and when they are not.

Did you check on someone today? Y / N

How did it go?

DATE:

What's going on?

Free write whatever you want, however you feel

Emotion vocabulary word: overwhelm

Meaning: to burden with too many tasks.

Overwhelm means the opposite of indifferent.

Example: "Do your little bit of good where you are; it's those little bits of good put together that overwhelm the world." — Desmond Tutu

Have you heard this word before? Y / N

Now that you know this feeling word, are there other words that you can think of that have a similar meaning?

Have you ever felt a sense of overwhelm? Y / N

What was going on?

It's ok to reach out when things are going well and when they are not.

Did you check on someone today? Y / N

How did it go?

DATE:

What's going on?

Free write whatever you want, however you feel

Did you move your body today?

N F T Z K E Q Q A S P I R I N G X U C W O
M W W V Z C N Y H X D I F F E R E N T F T
Q G Q T A D N Y I U I P M A D H E S I V E
R G T G P O W E R F U L H Y K R G N E E I
I O P T I M I S T I C B A G V Y U Q U Y L
H F E H N A D E D L K H N R R S R N U M B
N I O N E N M A R Y T I D N P D H R J X V
E M U E G Y S P U I R L S H N K W Q Y M S
R Z T G L C R N N N Y A O X A I X I Q J H
V H R A E W C N K G M R M M U I O N B T C
O A A T C C L O U D Y I E W S F U S O O X
U L G I T P F D I Y N O L L E G T I F B L
S T E V U Y T I L F P U Y W A O R D F S O
P I O E A J M P A L E S Q M T D A I E T K
G N U E L A S T I C F P R A E L G O N I C
P G S G J M E U A E L T Y L D Y E U D N A
Y O V E R W H E L M E D R E P H F S E A G
R I A U O U N L B K Z G P T D V B W D T E
I X W Q K B Q O E M N O S T A L G I C E Y
L S E F X J T Q M I N N O C E N T G T W Z
K R Z F N A S T Y E U Y K G A L R B M W K

Do you ever struggle to find your words?
Well find them here!!

6

NAUSEATED, OFFENDED, INNOCENT, HILARIOUS, OBSTINATE, OVERWHELMED, NUMB, DRUNK, OPTIMISTIC, NOSTALGIC, ADHESIVE, OUTRAGEOUS, NEGLECT, CLOUDY, ASPIRING, ELASTIC, LYING, INSIDIOUS, POWERFUL, DIFFERENT, NERVOUS, MALE, OUTRAGE, NASTY, CAGEY, GODLY, NEGATIVE, HANDSOMELY, PALE, HALTING

word search

Emotion vocabulary word: paranoid

Meaning: used to describe someone who has the mental disorder paranoia, which is characterized by delusions and feelings of suspicion, and being targeted by others. Such thoughts and actions can also be described as paranoid

Example: It is inappropriate to call someone paranoid when they are simply stating their lived experiences, and you have not had that same experience.

Have you heard this word before? Y / N

Now that you know this feeling word, are there other words that you can think of that have a similar meaning?

Have you ever felt paranoid? Y / N

What was going on?

It's ok to reach out when things are going well and when they are not.

Did you check on someone today? Y / N

How did it go?

DATE:

What's going on?

Free write whatever you want, however you feel

Emotion vocabulary word: pensive

Meaning: expressing or revealing thoughtfulness, usually marked by some sadness

Example: The child sat by themselves, looking pensive, after losing the match.

Have you heard this word before? Y / N

Now that you know this feeling word, are there other words that you can think of that have a similar meaning?

Have you ever felt pensive? Y / N

What was going on?

It's ok to reach out when things are going well and when they are not.

Did you check on someone today? Y / N

How did it go?

DATE:

What's going on?

Free write whatever you want, however you feel

Emotion vocabulary word: perplexed

Meaning: unable to understand something clearly or to think clearly

Example: The student was perplexed for a moment until he realized he was in the wrong classroom.

Have you heard this word before? Y / N

Now that you know this feeling word, are there other words that you can think of that have a similar meaning?

Have you ever felt perplexed? Y / N

What was going on?

It's ok to reach out when things are going well and when they are not.

Did you check on someone today? Y / N

How did it go?

DATE:

What's going on?

Free write whatever you want, however you feel

5 senses mindfullness exercise

This is a relaxation skill and coping tool for when you are stressed.
It works best if you practice this when you are relaxed (daily is preferable) so when / if you get stressed it's easy to recall.
If you do not practice this when you are relaxed it will be more difficult to remember what to do when you are stressed.
Try it now. Then try teaching a friend or family member.

5 things you can see
4 things you can hear
3 things you can touch
2 things you can smell
1 thing you can or would like to taste

Inhale slowly - then exhale.
Starting with the eyes, follow the steps above until you notice you are more present and relaxed.
Repeat if necessary.

Emotion vocabulary word: pessimism

Meaning: the tendency to see, anticipate, or emphasize only bad or undesirable outcomes, results, conditions, problems, etc.

Example: The runner struggled with a sense of pessimism after not running the fastest.

Have you heard this word before? Y / N

Now that you know this feeling word, are there other words that you can think of that have a similar meaning?

Have you ever experienced pessimism? Y / N

What was going on?

It's ok to reach out when things are going well and when they are not.

Did you check on someone today? Y / N

How did it go?

DATE:

What's going on?

Free write whatever you want, however you feel

Emotion vocabulary word: possessive

Meaning: jealously opposed to the personal independence of, or to any. influence other than one's own upon, a child, spouse, etc.

Example: Being in love is not the same as wanting to be possessive of someone.

Have you heard this word before? Y / N

Now that you know this feeling word, are there other words that you can think of that have a similar meaning?

Have you ever felt possessive? Y / N

What was going on?

It's ok to reach out when things are going well and when they are not.

Did you check on someone today? Y / N

How did it go?

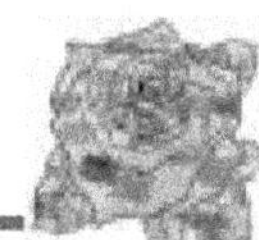

DATE:

What's going on?

Free write whatever you want, however you feel

P T Y U P Y G Z H I P L U P I D I O T I C
M C W F L J U I P U A X R O V D R U N K L
V P F P E S W F A K R P E S S I M I S M L
R Y P O A J S E S F A F V I L I L N D F Y
G H E W S N H M S M N D M T W Q N N U T I
M X R E E E H I I A O S B I U U O S P T N
U K P R D T I V O L I G O V U M W Q C E G
M Q L L R R L C N E D Y E E N L C A G E Y
F Q E E S W A C L O U D Y K P P V H A P W
V K X S T D R P O L I T E N E S S O B J E
P K E S Y F I R S T F L Z S Y K J X C Z E
A M D W A M O N Q P E R S E V E R I N G P
T Q G Q U U U X I N S I D I O U S P L Y Y
I P O S S E S S I V E V G F Z V H Y B O I
E X Q C P L E A S U R E T Q W P A L D P S
N I N Q U I S I T I V E V F L Y L T W A Z
C F C X N K B P U Z Z L E D D C T Y P L H
E A I M O U P A N I C K E D J A I C R E J
M E G C R T E W S P I T Y X V H N Z I L Z
P U F T E B J Z N E B U L O U S G P D P W
D P E N S I V E N E S S H R C A X E E J Y

**Do you ever struggle to find your words?
Well find them here!!**

7

LYING, PRIDE, INQUISITIVE, POWERLESS, FIRST, CLOUDY, HALTING, PATIENCE, POLITENESS, PITY, PALE, PASSION, POSITIVE, HILARIOUS, PARANOID, PLEASED, CAGEY, PERPLEXED, IDIOTIC, DRUNK, PENSIVENESS, POSSESSIVE, INSIDIOUS, PUZZLED, PANICKED, PLEASURE, MALE, NEBULOUS, PERSEVERING, PESSIMISM

word search

Emotion vocabulary word: rash

Meaning: acting or tending to act too hastily or without due consideration. Rash means the opposite of deliberate.

Example: While arguing, they made the rash decision to breakup. But weeks later they both regretted it.

Have you heard this word before? Y / N

Now that you know this feeling word, are there other words that you can think of that have a similar meaning?

Have you ever acted in a rash manner? Y / N

What was going on?

It's ok to reach out when things are going well and when they are not.

Did you check on someone today? Y / N

How did it go?

DATE:

What's going on?

Free write whatever you want, however you feel

Practice the 5 senses exercise

Emotion vocabulary word: rattled

Meaning: to upset especially to the point of loss of poise and composure.

Example: The sudden death of the school's principal rattled the students and many students stayed home for several days to grieve.

Have you heard this word before? Y / N

Now that you know this feeling word, are there other words that you can think of that have a similar meaning?

Have you ever felt rattled? Y / N

What was going on?

It's ok to reach out when things are going well and when they are not.

Did you check on someone today? Y / N

How did it go?

DATE:

What's going on?

Free write whatever you want, however you feel

Emotion vocabulary word: reluctant

Meaning: showing doubt or unwillingness

Example: The Tuskegee study, and countless other atrocities, have led many Black people to be reluctant of the American medical system.

Have you heard this word before? Y / N

Now that you know this feeling word, are there other words that you can think of that have a similar meaning?

Have you ever been reluctant? Y / N

What was going on?

It's ok to reach out when things are going well and when they are not.

Did you check on someone today? Y / N

How did it go?

DATE:

What's going on?

Free write whatever you want, however you feel

Emotion vocabulary word: resentment

Meaning: the feeling of displeasure or indignation at some act, remark, person, etc., regarded as causing injury or insult.

Example: The students expressed resentment at the sexist dress code by protesting and refusing to attend classes.

Have you heard this word before? Y / N

Now that you know this feeling word, are there other words that you can think of that have a similar meaning?

Have you ever felt resentment? Y / N

What was going on?

It's ok to reach out when things are going well and when they are not.

Did you check on someone today? Y / N

How did it go?

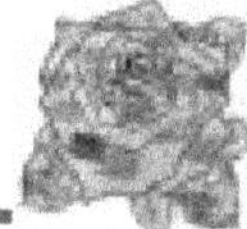

DATE:

What's going on?

Free write whatever you want, however you feel

BREATHE

THE NOUN EXERCISE

This is a relaxation skill and coping tool for when you are stressed.
It works best if you practice this when you are relaxed (daily is preferable) so when / if you get stressed it's easy to recall.
If you do not practice this when you are relaxed it will be more difficult to remember what to do when you are stressed.
Try it now. Then try teaching a friend or family member.

Is there something,

a person,

place or

thing,

real or imagined

that whenever you think of it - it

brings you joy, peace,

happiness...?

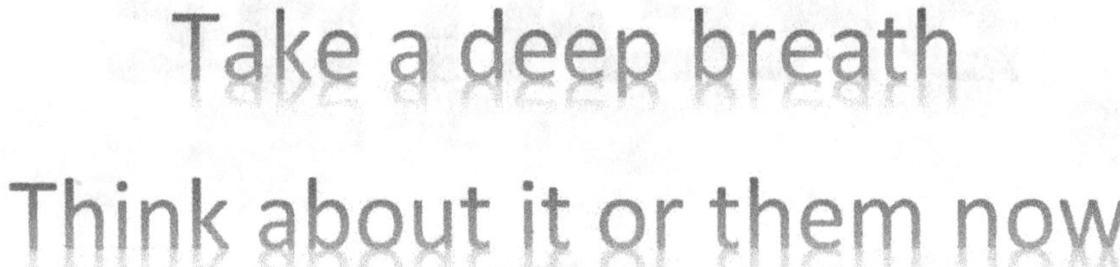

Emotion vocabulary word: resignation

Meaning: the feeling of a person who is prepared to accept something unpleasant.

Example: "The truth is, I've never been a big believer in destiny. I worry that it encourages resignation in the down-and-out and complacency among the powerful." — Barack Obama

Have you heard this word before? Y / N

Now that you know this feeling word, are there other words that you can think of that have a similar meaning?

Have you ever experienced resignation? Y / N

What was going on?

It's ok to reach out when things are going well and when they are not.

Did you check on someone today? Y / N

How did it go?

DATE:

What's going on?

Free write whatever you want, however you feel

Emotion vocabulary word: revulsion

Meaning: a strong feeling of disgust, distaste, or dislike.

Example: "It's funny about 'passing [for white].' We disapprove of it and at the same time condone it. It excites our contempt and yet we rather admire it. We shy away from it with an odd kind of revulsion, but we protect it." —Nella Larsen

Have you heard this word before? Y / N

Now that you know this feeling word, are there other words that you can think of that have a similar meaning?

Have you ever felt revulsion? Y / N

What was going on?

It's ok to reach out when things are going well and when they are not.

Did you check on someone today? Y / N

How did it go?

DATE:

What's going on?

Free write whatever you want, however you feel

I K I C G T N E M K T L M L H O Q P S X O O

B N P A R T E L J C Z I D I O T I C S U L U

Z E O A E F J A Y D G V B E U C G C U P C E

W B W H A N D S O M E L Y Q V J D J O T D T

V U E R A S H T H B O Z A H W I A I O P Q G

T L R B M V M I F Z H O H F S A H N Z S K D

H O F D A M J C Y I I A Q S J P B S J A R I

I U U I T A R E L A X E D V V P R I N D E L

L S L F U D R E S I G N A T I O N D R J S S

A Y Z F R H B W R E L I E V E D R I P O T P

R W L E E E R E L U C T A N T J E O R L L I

I A J R R S Q C T Q K L P T R C S U E D E J

O X C E A I R E G R E T A Y A N E S V M S Y

U A F N R V G W R V V K L E T F N F U A S R

S E F T E E P G U D P S E Z T I T Z L L N E

K I N Q U I S I T I V E C Q L R M S S E E J

H U Q D G U U Q H O B X W O E S E I I N S E

C L O U D Y D N L D X K Z L D T N X O A S C

R E M O R S E J E V Z O G Q C Q T X N C I T

F W N S K D I T S D U Q L L Y I N G W D L E

Q M W C R A G E S I G D C P L K B B H G V D

B Q X L F C K Q S U Q S D K D J E G V Q T Z

DO YOU EVER STRUGGLE TO FIND YOUR WORDS?
WELL FIND THEM HERE!!

8

MALE, PALE, RUTHLESS, RELUCTANT, ADHESIVE, REGRET, INQUISITIVE, INSIDIOUS, RELIEVED, RASH, RELAXED, FIRST, HILARIOUS, LYING, RESENTMENT, CLOUDY, DIFFERENT, IDIOTIC, RESIGNATION, REVULSION, REJECTED, MATURE, RATTLED, POWERFUL, NEBULOUS, REMORSE, ELASTIC, RAGE, HANDSOMELY, RESTLESSNESS

word search

Emotion vocabulary word: serene

Meaning: calm, peaceful, or tranquil

Example: His grandparent's backyard garden was so serene, he almost forgot that he was in the middle of a large city.

Have you heard this word before? Y / N

Now that you know this feeling word, are there other words that you can think of that have a similar meaning?

Have you ever felt serene? Y / N

What was going on?

It's ok to reach out when things are going well and when they are not.

Did you check on someone today? Y / N

How did it go?

DATE:

What's going on?

Free write whatever you want, however you feel

Take a deep breath and think of the person, place or thing that always bring you joy

Emotion vocabulary word: smug

Meaning: highly self-satisfied.

Example: The calculus tutor was very intelligent, but they were so smug no one wanted to learn from them.

Have you heard this word before? Y / N

Now that you know this feeling word, are there other words that you can think of that have a similar meaning?

Have you ever felt or known anyone who was smug? Y / N

What was going on?

It's ok to reach out when things are going well and when they are not.

Did you check on someone today? Y / N

How did it go?

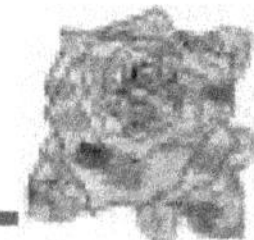

DATE:

What's going on?

Free write whatever you want, however you feel

Emotion vocabulary word: suspense

Meaning: mental uncertainty; may be pleasant or unpleasant.

Example: The suspense builds as the story progresses.

Have you heard this word before? Y / N

Now that you know this feeling word, are there other words that you can think of that have a similar meaning?

Have you ever experienced suspense? Y / N

What was going on?

It's ok to reach out when things are going well and when they are not.

Did you check on someone today? Y / N

How did it go?

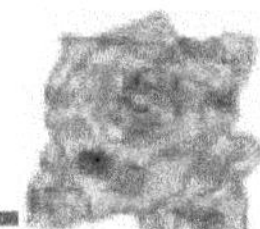

DATE:

What's going on?

Free write whatever you want, however you feel

L S U S P I C I O U S R A S S Q K O E N X Q J
A S B S R A N H K W S N Y B U E R Z L T H Q J
Z U A E M S S Y M P A T H Y B X D O H S M T O
S L C D F C B P B T D B R K M H Q U O F Q N B
H L D V H A L I D P N J D V I L Z Q Q F J T D
A E K E D R N E O C E R Y Q S E R E N I T Y G
M N B Y M E S V U G S I K X S D S L S I J H T
E N O Q S D U L V X S J I W I M C B R E X U S
G E H R T U R C Z I Z S T Q V G O I G V L O P
V S W B R S P C E L B L Q Y E V R A G U X F I
B S X P O M R S U F F E R I N G N L E T W M T
W E X P N C I N J C S T U C K I V B I O E Y E
G U S P G H S L L T H G V X M H D X E C L Y R
I Q H H T F E A C W S J N N Q S A T S L H A V
L R A O S N Z S U S P E N S E O K N H T D W M
V B M J P X P E F Y W U Z H B R W D O V X N W
D K E E P U N S O Z F S M U G R T B C A U D J
V F L Q G C K V U B Y Z B H C O L Z K H K Y N
G I E O S T R E S S E D L B U W G X E Q R Q J
T B S I N X R S C H A D E N F R E U D E I H R
I I S X H R G E Z Y S T U B B O R N Z O H O J
L S U Q S A T I S F A C T I O N I E Y E V R Z
Z C E E E T W X Y C J S E N T I M E N T A L G

Do you ever struggle to find your words?
Well find them here!!

9

STUCK, SHOCKED, SURPRISE, SUBMISSIVE, SULLENNESS, SUFFERING, SHAMELESS, SCORN, SYMPATHY, SATISFACTION, SUSPICIOUS, SADNESS, SCARED, SCHADENFREUDE, STRESSED, SERENITY, STUBBORN, SMUG, SHAME, SORROW, SUSPENSE, STRONG, SPITE, SENTIMENTAL

word search

Emotion vocabulary word: tenderness

Meaning: gentleness and affection.

Example: The new parents held their twins with tenderness.

Have you heard this word before? Y / N

Now that you know this feeling word, are there other words that you can think of that have a similar meaning?

Have you ever felt tenderness? Y / N

What was going on?

It's ok to reach out when things are going well and when they are not.

Did you check on someone today? Y / N

How did it go?

DATE:

What's going on?

Free write whatever you want, however you feel

Emotion vocabulary word: torment

Meaning: something that causes great bodily or mental pain or suffering.

Example: The mother felt torment when her child became ill.

Have you heard this word before? Y / N

Now that you know this feeling word, are there other words that you can think of that have a similar meaning?

Have you ever felt torment? Y / N

What was going on?

It's ok to reach out when things are going well and when they are not.

Did you check on someone today? Y / N

How did it go?

DATE:

What's going on?

Free write whatever you want, however you feel

Emotion vocabulary word: triumphant ▲

Meaning: having achieved victory or success.

Example: Serena Williams ended her triumphant 27-year tennis career at the 2022 US Open.

Have you heard this word before? Y / N

Now that you know this feeling word, are there other words that you can think of that have a similar meaning?

Have you ever felt triumphant? Y / N

What was going on?

It's ok to reach out when things are going well and when they are not.

Did you check on someone today? Y / N

How did it go?

DATE:

What's going on?

Free write whatever you want, however you feel

B Q U G K P R F I A K D T M S S L E Z B W Z
E B C H K A L S L L O I E T H R I L L E D C
C U Q H I L A R I O U S N B F K U A F D E S
S U J J R M Y U Q G J C S Z I U K S J W E N
N E B U L O U S Q W E R I N V T P T T I I E
L L D I F F E R E N T E O H U I O I R E N C
I L Q Z C B E H C U L E N P C W W C I V Q H
I C W Q W W I C L M A T U R E E E C U N U U
C T D X H E D H O Q S N F D J E R G M Z I B
O L Q A T L I W U O Y E D Q G K F I P W S B
C Y I Y F I O T D R U N K H D S U D H Z I Y
A I N L L I T R Y T O R M E N T L L A L T O
V N S B A N I O M V W V R S N Y E D N S I H
A G I Z M N C U C Q Q K I A J X K I T N V V
I S D A D O L B T I R E D D M G X Q E E E I
L U I P E C N L T H A N K F U L N E S S U T
A R O T Y E A E Z A X H O U T R A G E O U S
B X U E G N O D O S Z V F G M G R C Y T N W
L U S R D T T O L E R A N C E F Y P Z R P S
E L S R R B T E N D E R N E S S N O O U M F
R Z K O T J X C W C L W O A D C H S E S Z B
I M E R E Z F P O B Y U N O F H F E U T M W

10

DO YOU EVER STRUGGLE TO FIND YOUR WORDS?
WELL FIND THEM HERE!!

MERE, ELASTIC, TIRED, NEBULOUS, INNOCENT, TROUBLED, TRUST, DRUNK, THANKFULNESS, TOLERANCE, THRILLED, CHUBBY, HILARIOUS, INQUISITIVE, CLOUDY, DISCREET, AVAILABLE, TERROR, INSIDIOUS, TENDERNESS, TRIUMPHANT, POWERFUL, IDIOTIC, TORMENT, OUTRAGEOUS, DIFFERENT, TENSION, LYING, MATURE, SAD

word search

Emotion vocabulary word: undermine

Meaning: to weaken secretly or little by little

Example: Both the struggling students and the most gifted ones are receiving limited support from an undermined educational system.

Have you heard this word before? Y / N

Now that you know this feeling word, are there other words that you can think of that have a similar meaning?

Have you ever felt undermined? Y / N

What was going on?

It's ok to reach out when things are going well and when they are not.

Did you check on someone today? Y / N

How did it go?

DATE:

What's going on?

Free write whatever you want, however you feel

Emotion vocabulary word: vengeful

Meaning: seeking revenge. The act of inflicting hurt or harm on someone for an injury or wrongdoing suffered at their hands.

Example: The robbery was committed by a vengeful former employee.

Have you heard this word before? Y / N

Now that you know this feeling word, are there other words that you can think of that have a similar meaning?

Have you ever felt vengeful? Y / N

What was going on?

It's ok to reach out when things are going well and when they are not.

Did you check on someone today? Y / N

How did it go?

DATE:

What's going on?

Free write whatever you want, however you feel

Take in a slow deep breath, then exhale just as slowly. How do you feel?
Pick specific colors for this coloring sheet. Which colors did you select? Why?

Mindfulness Coloring

Practice deep breathing

Emotion vocabulary word: vicious

Meaning: dangerously aggressive

Example: Debt can lead borrowers to take out another one loan to pay off the previous one, leading them into a vicious cycle that only profits the person who owns their debt.

Have you heard this word before? Y / N

Now that you know this feeling word, are there other words that you can think of that have a similar meaning?

Have you ever felt vicious? Y / N

What was going on?

It's ok to reach out when things are going well and when they are not.

Did you check on someone today? Y / N

How did it go?

DATE:

What's going on?

Free write whatever you want, however you feel

Emotion vocabulary word: vigilance

Meaning: the quality or state of staying alert especially to possible danger

Example: One cannot relax or rest if one is always forced to be vigilant.

Have you heard this word before? Y / N

Now that you know this feeling word, are there other words that you can think of that have a similar meaning?

Have you ever dealt with vigilance? Y / N

What was going on?

It's ok to reach out when things are going well and when they are not.

Did you check on someone today? Y / N

How did it go?

DATE:

What's going on?

Free write whatever you want, however you feel

Emotion vocabulary word: vulnerable

Meaning: willing to show emotion or to allow one's weaknesses to be seen or known.

Example: The patriarchy also hurts men and boys as they are rarely seen as vulnerable.

Have you heard this word before? Y / N

Now that you know this feeling word, are there other words that you can think of that have a similar meaning?

Have you ever felt or been vulnerable? Y / N

What was going on?

It's ok to reach out when things are going well and when they are not.

Did you check on someone today? Y / N

How did it go?

DATE:

What's going on?

Free write whatever you want, however you feel

Emotion vocabulary word: woe

Meaning: grievous distress, affliction, or trouble.

Example: Instead of apologizing, the accuser took a woe-is-me attitude, which thankfully no one believed.

Have you heard this word before? Y / N

Now that you know this feeling word, are there other words that you can think of that have a similar meaning?

Have you ever experienced a feeling of woe? Y / N

What was going on?

It's ok to reach out when things are going well and when they are not.

Did you check on someone today? Y / N

How did it go?

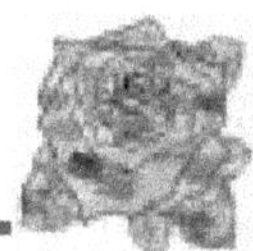

DATE:

What's going on?

Free write whatever you want, however you feel

B K S F P Z L I Z V U L N E R A B L E O K

U X Z U D Q M D I U N S E T T L E D K A Q

T Y Z W E A K I J E G I U O J C X G H Z E

I K R I N D U O U A M N N T F S W R A T H

H T Y N Z H E T N W U Q N A I T S M A L E

S A I S S K G I D O N U E D R I L X U C P

V I G I L A N C E R C I R H S L N J N P P

N P A D V C W G R R E S V E T P A L E F X

J R P I O O O O M I R I E S G C G H A H S

N X O O L V R O I E T T D I V J D I S H R

A R T U Q B T V N D A I P V J J M L I P B

L U P S E T H L E R I V U E A K V A N P A

C L O U D Y Y C D H N E P J H V K R E V C

H A N D S O M E L Y T U A S Y X M I S W K

Y U K Z O F G O D L Y Q W U Q G P O S Y C

I N G I O Z C L K T I P O W E R F U L D W

W H N P H T P Q K P T Q X L M U M S T Z D

O A V Z S H A L T I N G A N W H W Q T Y D

E P N U H S P X O V E N G E F U L S S G S

R P C A P P S W G E V I C I O U S V G O K

F Y J A X B U O F U N S U R E V S U I S R

**DO YOU EVER STRUGGLE TO FIND YOUR WORDS?
WELL FIND THEM HERE!!**

11

ADHESIVE, VIGILANCE, HALTING, GODLY, UNCERTAINTY, POWERFUL, UNDERMINED, VICIOUS, IDIOTIC, WOE, HILARIOUS, WORTHY, PALE, UNEASINESS, CLOUDY, UNSURE, HANDSOMELY, UNSETTLED, FIRST, UNNERVED, WEAK, INSIDIOUS, VENGEFUL, WRATH, WORRIED, UNHAPPY, MALE, UPSET, INQUISITIVE, VULNERABLE

word search

Emotion vocabulary word: worthy ▲

Meaning: having enough value or excellence

Example: It is often difficult for the oppressed to feel worthy.

Have you heard this word before? Y / N

Now that you know this feeling word, are there other words that you can think of that have a similar meaning?

When did or do you feel most worthy?

It's ok to reach out when things are going well and when they are not.

Did you check on someone today? Y / N

How did it go?

DATE:

What's going on?

Free write whatever you want, however you feel

Take a deep breath and think about what brings you peace

It's worth repeating:

Feelings are not facts, but feelings (your feelings and the feelings of others) are to be heard and respected.

"I feel…" statements: feeling + event or issue + solution

Listening is just as important as learning about feeling words and expressing feelings.

consent, boundaries and safety are reciprocal (give and receive)

Sensations: Notice how your body feels when you're around certain people.

Breath = life: take a second before you ask or while hearing an emotionally heavy question.

Coping skills: practice these as much as possible so they become habit.

Additional support may be found at: therapyforblackmen.com and (BEAM) Black Emotional and Mental Health Collective (https://beam.community)

All emotions are valid.

Example: Anger is a valid and useful emotion

But it is not ok to harm someone because of your anger.

word search

SOLUTIONS

A	B	O	A	P	O	M	X	C	F	I	X	J	K	W	S	W	H	R	J	W	R	A
U	G	Q	F	M	Z	H	A	G	I	T	A	T	I	O	N	E	K	Q	F	Y	S	N
R	H	K	G	L	G	N	O	Y	T	M	A	S	T	O	N	I	S	H	E	D	S	N
U	I	V	X	A	F	R	A	I	D	F	S	K	A	M	N	B	X	P	A	S	P	O
A	Y	I	A	E	A	B	E	R	Y	A	L	A	R	M	E	D	H	P	D	P	C	Y
V	B	E	A	N	T	I	C	I	P	A	T	I	N	G	A	A	W	Q	M	Z	R	E
Y	U	N	B	O	J	R	M	P	P	G	B	X	Z	S	N	A	K	M	I	Z	T	D
A	J	E	S	L	P	D	X	J	Y	N	I	B	P	N	G	C	O	I	R	R	B	L
S	D	A	P	P	R	E	H	E	N	S	I	O	N	Q	E	D	B	R	A	C	Q	R
S	J	B	A	A	S	A	A	G	U	A	G	I	H	F	R	N	B	D	T	A	Q	A
E	N	A	R	M	F	W	P	I	L	Y	R	A	L	I	E	N	A	T	I	O	N	D
R	H	V	R	A	I	E	A	Q	C	V	L	Z	A	L	A	R	M	Z	O	R	W	Y
T	H	E	O	Z	I	S	T	A	L	A	T	T	E	N	T	I	V	E	N	E	S	S
I	T	R	G	E	J	L	H	D	N	B	V	R	N	M	G	M	L	U	G	A	A	W
V	X	S	A	M	R	Z	Y	O	A	C	C	E	P	T	A	N	C	E	J	T	F	X
E	W	I	N	E	I	U	O	R	A	M	B	I	V	A	L	E	N	C	E	T	F	R
E	K	O	T	N	J	J	K	A	A	G	G	R	E	S	S	I	V	E	T	R	E	S
W	Q	N	P	T	I	E	Y	T	N	U	A	M	U	S	E	M	E	N	T	A	C	O
A	A	N	X	I	O	U	S	I	G	A	X	W	D	S	Z	V	Y	A	P	C	T	R
F	H	K	I	J	E	C	S	O	U	P	W	E	G	T	S	U	D	G	K	T	I	J
Q	E	E	N	F	M	A	X	N	I	O	C	V	V	J	F	F	S	O	M	I	O	O
B	U	I	M	H	T	A	D	N	S	X	S	Z	V	Y	N	X	O	N	L	O	N	O
Y	F	R	T	K	R	Z	B	I	H	W	H	F	L	K	U	U	Q	Y	Z	N	U	V

1

AGGRESSIVE, ALIENATION, ATTRACTION, APATHY, ACCEPTANCE, ALARMED, ANGUISH, ADORATION, ANXIOUS, ANGER, APPREHENSION, ASTONISHED, AFFECTION, AVERSION, ANTICIPATING, ATTENTIVENESS, AMAZEMENT, ARROGANT, AFRAID, ADMIRATION, AMUSEMENT, AWE, ALARM, AMBIVALENCE, ASSERTIVE, AGONY, AGITATION, ANNOYED

word search

Solution

D	P	Z	N	W	Y	M	A	D	E	T	E	R	M	I	N	E	D	J	Q	T	X
I	O	W	U	S	B	D	X	D	I	S	P	L	E	A	S	U	R	E	D	W	U
S	D	I	S	O	R	I	E	N	T	E	D	A	D	D	U	O	S	C	I	C	Z
P	R	G	D	D	I	S	G	U	S	T	I	D	I	E	A	O	U	G	S	X	U
I	E	X	U	A	D	C	A	A	W	D	S	I	S	M	Z	D	S	D	G	A	E
R	A	J	D	K	I	O	M	D	E	U	C	S	C	O	V	D	Y	I	R	T	D
I	D	D	I	B	S	M	U	G	V	M	O	H	O	R	A	C	S	S	U	H	J
T	L	Z	S	G	M	F	J	X	M	B	M	E	N	A	S	A	D	B	N	D	I
E	I	C	T	U	A	O	A	V	Q	S	B	A	T	L	B	U	E	E	T	R	S
D	L	Y	R	Z	Y	R	J	N	Q	T	O	R	E	I	N	K	J	L	L	I	B
W	B	F	E	A	S	T	I	T	L	R	B	T	N	Z	F	D	E	I	E	V	W
O	D	I	S	T	U	R	B	E	D	U	U	E	T	E	J	I	C	E	D	E	N
W	D	I	S	L	I	K	E	O	Z	C	L	N	M	D	A	S	T	F	B	N	D
D	E	P	R	E	S	S	E	D	Q	K	A	E	E	P	H	T	I	K	V	K	E
Z	G	C	H	K	K	O	D	T	Q	B	T	D	N	A	E	R	O	A	B	H	S
O	N	M	C	A	W	I	A	Z	D	L	E	K	T	L	D	A	N	S	W	R	P
A	R	B	W	S	B	D	Z	Q	G	H	D	J	N	Z	O	C	R	I	E	D	A
D	E	L	I	G	H	T	E	D	W	R	X	E	H	K	U	T	L	V	Y	I	I
U	B	V	S	M	T	N	D	P	B	H	J	S	F	H	B	I	L	J	S	G	R
C	I	D	I	S	A	P	P	O	I	N	T	M	E	N	T	O	H	R	R	U	L
N	D	E	S	I	R	E	F	G	B	U	A	B	Z	D	F	N	Z	E	U	V	R
K	C	M	D	D	O	M	I	N	A	N	T	I	P	S	N	H	U	C	E	L	E

2

DREAD, DISTRESS, DISCOMBOBULATED, DEMORALIZED, DESIRE, DOMINANT, DISBELIEF, DETERMINED, DISGUST, DRIVEN, DESPAIR, DISTRACTION, DISLIKE, DISCONTENTMENT, DISAPPOINTMENT, DUMBSTRUCK, DAZED, DEPRESSED, DISPIRITED, DOUBT, DISPLEASURE, DISORIENTED, DISTURBED, DISMAY, DELIGHTED, DISHEARTENED, DEJECTION, DISCOMFORT, DISGRUNTLED

vitdoamet	=	motivated	senadniugnrtd	=	understanding	ptiy	=	pity
nepcgteirs	=	respecting	osnccusoi	=	conscious	lefs	=	self
iatglhon	=	loathing	lcaictri	=	critical	narcgi	=	caring

SOLUTIONS

word scramble

3

SOLUTION

C	J	Q	C	C	Z	V	I	C	R	U	E	L	T	Y	N	H	I	T	J	G
Y	B	F	Z	U	A	C	L	A	U	S	T	R	O	P	H	O	B	I	C	G
N	I	I	Z	V	L	L	H	M	B	H	S	P	J	C	O	N	T	E	N	T
I	L	R	L	H	U	S	P	Y	A	J	C	O	N	T	E	M	P	T	F	K
C	I	W	P	G	N	K	J	B	F	W	H	N	G	C	O	U	R	A	G	E
I	B	R	O	O	D	I	N	G	F	U	M	H	V	E	Y	S	Q	V	J	H
S	Q	F	I	A	C	B	N	N	L	C	O	M	F	O	R	T	A	B	L	E
M	Z	P	V	F	V	E	Y	N	E	B	R	A	Z	E	N	P	G	J	Y	K
C	A	X	M	I	R	W	F	Z	D	Y	Q	C	O	N	F	U	S	I	O	N
S	Z	O	E	C	C	I	W	X	C	A	R	I	N	G	H	K	H	C	O	J
X	V	N	H	H	G	L	I	C	O	M	P	A	S	S	I	O	N	O	N	K
L	O	N	C	E	D	D	Q	R	R	G	Z	A	E	W	N	K	Z	E	R	J
C	S	O	A	E	C	E	C	D	D	E	L	Y	H	K	E	C	C	R	H	B
B	C	V	R	R	H	R	H	G	K	M	O	D	L	C	A	L	M	C	R	N
N	A	P	E	F	A	E	E	Y	S	V	F	U	H	Y	B	Q	S	I	X	H
B	R	B	L	U	R	D	E	C	O	W	A	R	D	L	Y	G	M	V	L	K
A	E	B	E	L	I	X	K	J	V	M	B	C	O	N	F	I	D	E	N	T
Q	F	Z	S	N	T	S	Y	I	U	N	O	C	U	R	I	O	S	I	T	Y
Q	R	Y	S	E	Y	Z	K	G	K	P	R	D	Z	F	P	B	L	I	S	S
N	E	O	N	S	N	Q	N	F	F	Y	E	B	A	B	I	T	T	E	R	M
M	E	S	J	S	F	X	M	D	O	Q	D	H	Y	E	K	G	W	L	X	M

word search

4

CHEEKY, CARING, BAFFLED, CRUELTY, BRAZEN,

CALM, COMFORTABLE, COWARDLY, CHARITY,

BORED, CONTENT, CHEERFULNESS, COERCIVE,

CONFIDENT, COMPASSION, CONTEMPT, CURIOSITY,

CONFUSION, BITTER, CYNICISM, BLISS, CAREFREE,

CARELESS, BEWILDERED, CLAUSTROPHOBIC,

BROODING, COURAGE

K I N S I D I O U S I A D Q E N Z C I U A
M Z Y T N I D I O T I C G G F B G C I T H
A B S L Q H M I S E R A B L E C P E G C M
X J R D U U K N M I X E D _ U P A S X S K
Q F U Z I H I L A R I O U S M H L P W F C
P A M B S Q B O M W N Q J X O V E I F H A
M S C T I H F N I M O O D Y R O P M I R G
E Y J L T H O G S A E U R L T U A H R L E
L D B M I U P I E E U N V S I V S Y S W Y
A E Z O V A L N R I S K Z Q F L U S T Q F
N M A D E B O G L M O E A U I Z W M V X V
C W Q E A S N Y I Y D V Z Q E E L N G P B
H L U S T H E I N S M F Y V D K I E B O Y
O T T T E A L Y E T V D L O O P Y B P W O
L O R Y I L Y A S I F R E L X K Z U W E R
Y H I O B T Z S S F D U N O W O J L R R Q
D M L I K I N G J I C N S V C N X O V F F
A A X V F N W N O E G K V E N U N U R U W
A L F U H G G D L D E C L O U D Y S L L W
A E S K U L A Z Y O I B I E S R N F H E V
L O A T H I N G V O X G T P U W W V O E U

SOLUTIONS

5

CAGEY, HALTING, LAZY, MORTIFIED, LONELY, IDIOTIC, LONGING, LOVE, PALE, MALE, NEBULOUS, MYSTIFIED, LOATHING, LOOPY, LUST, MELANCHOLY, INQUISITIVE, MISERLINESS, DRUNK, FIRST, HILARIOUS, MAD, POWERFUL, MISERABLE, MIXED UP, INSIDIOUS, LIKING, CLOUDY, MOODY, MODESTY

word search

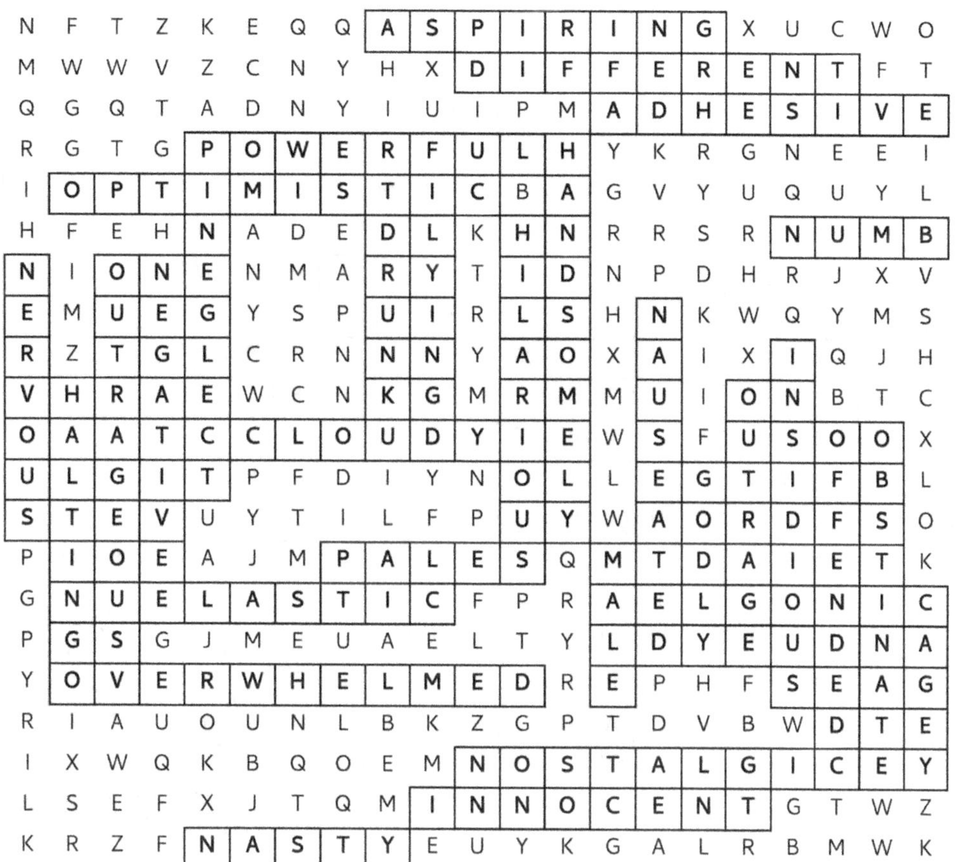

SOLUTIONS

6

NAUSEATED, OFFENDED, INNOCENT, HILARIOUS, OBSTINATE, OVERWHELMED, NUMB, DRUNK, OPTIMISTIC, NOSTALGIC, ADHESIVE, OUTRAGEOUS, NEGLECT, CLOUDY, ASPIRING, ELASTIC, LYING, INSIDIOUS, POWERFUL, DIFFERENT, NERVOUS, MALE, OUTRAGE, NASTY, CAGEY, GODLY, NEGATIVE, HANDSOMELY, PALE, HALTING

word search

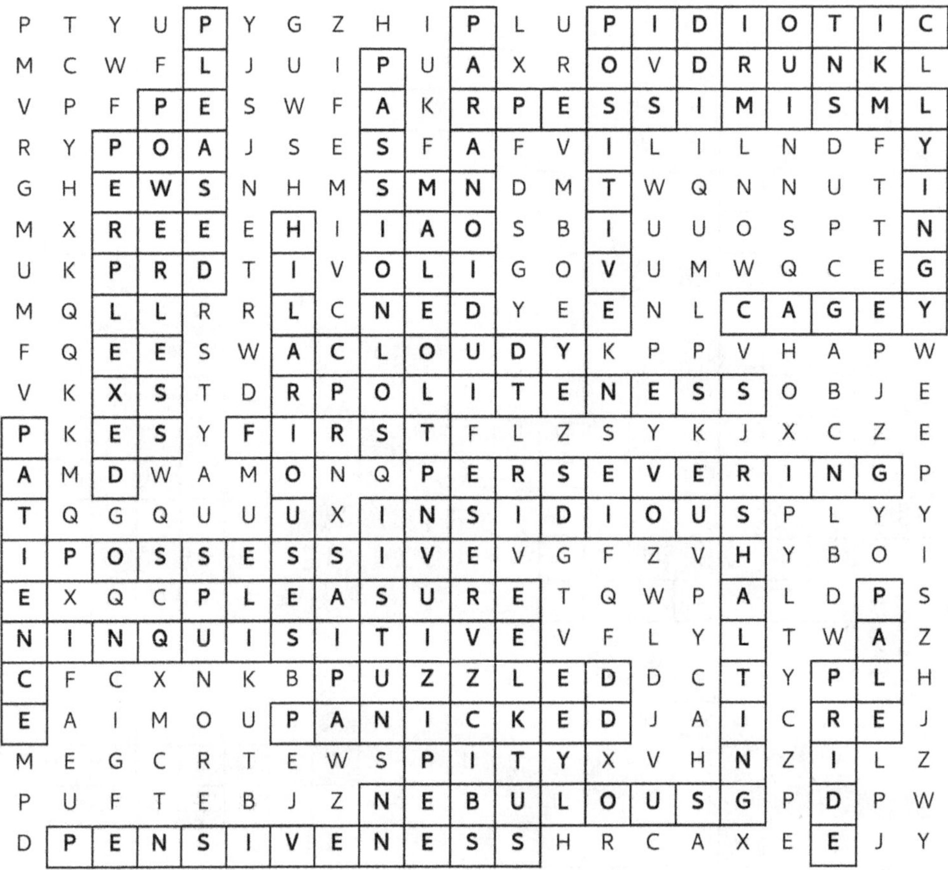

SOLUTIONS

7

LYING, PRIDE, INQUISITIVE, POWERLESS, FIRST, CLOUDY, HALTING, PATIENCE, POLITENESS, PITY, PALE, PASSION, POSITIVE, HILARIOUS, PARANOID, PLEASED, CAGEY, PERPLEXED, IDIOTIC, DRUNK, PENSIVENESS, POSSESSIVE, INSIDIOUS, PUZZLED, PANICKED, PLEASURE, MALE, NEBULOUS, PERSEVERING, PESSIMISM

word search

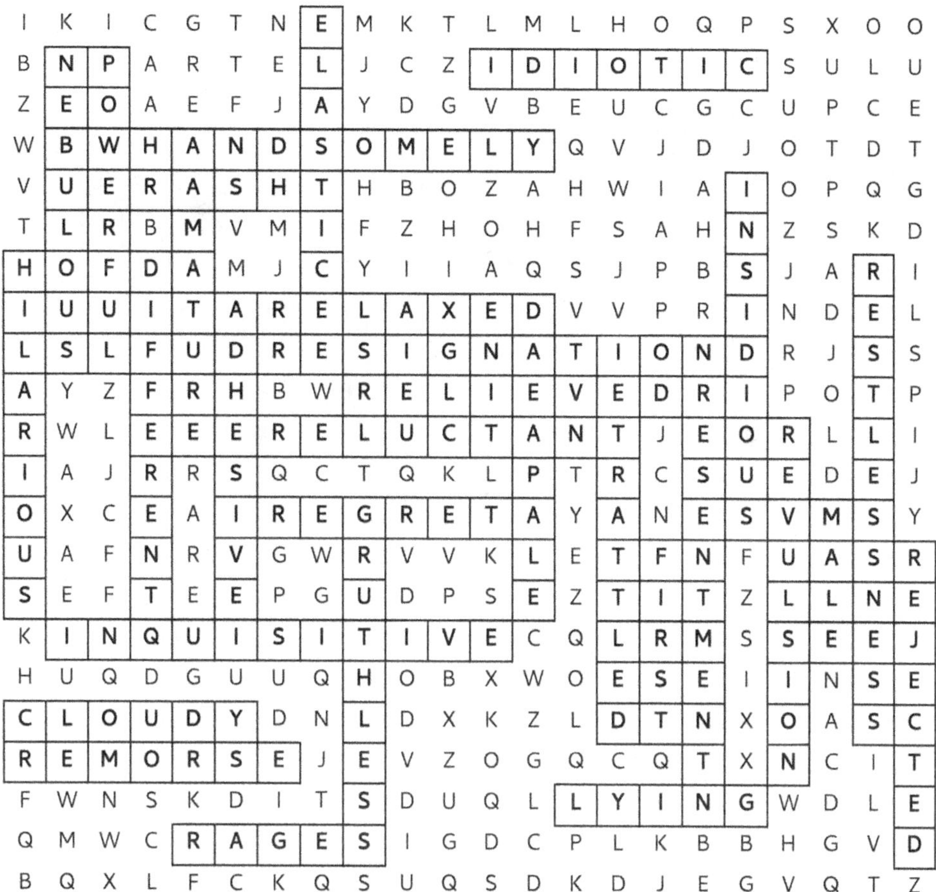

SOLUTIONS

8

MALE, PALE, RUTHLESS, RELUCTANT, ADHESIVE, REGRET, INQUISITIVE, INSIDIOUS, RELIEVED, RASH, RELAXED, FIRST, HILARIOUS, LYING, RESENTMENT, CLOUDY, DIFFERENT, IDIOTIC, RESIGNATION, REVULSION, REJECTED, MATURE, RATTLED, POWERFUL, NEBULOUS, REMORSE, ELASTIC, RAGE, HANDSOMELY, RESTLESSNESS

word search

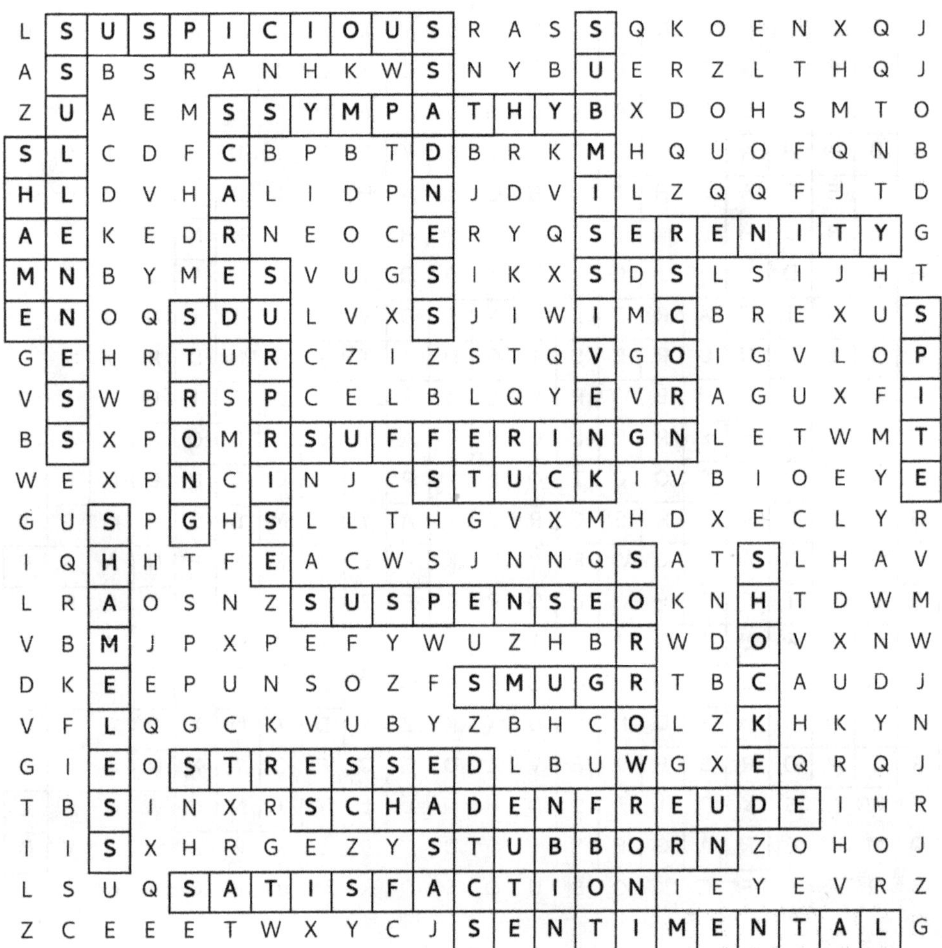

SOLUTIONS

9

STUCK, SHOCKED, SURPRISE, SUBMISSIVE, SULLENNESS, SUFFERING, SHAMELESS, SCORN, SYMPATHY, SATISFACTION, SUSPICIOUS, SADNESS, SCARED, SCHADENFREUDE, STRESSED, SERENITY, STUBBORN, SMUG, SHAME, SORROW, SUSPENSE, STRONG, SPITE, SENTIMENTAL

word search

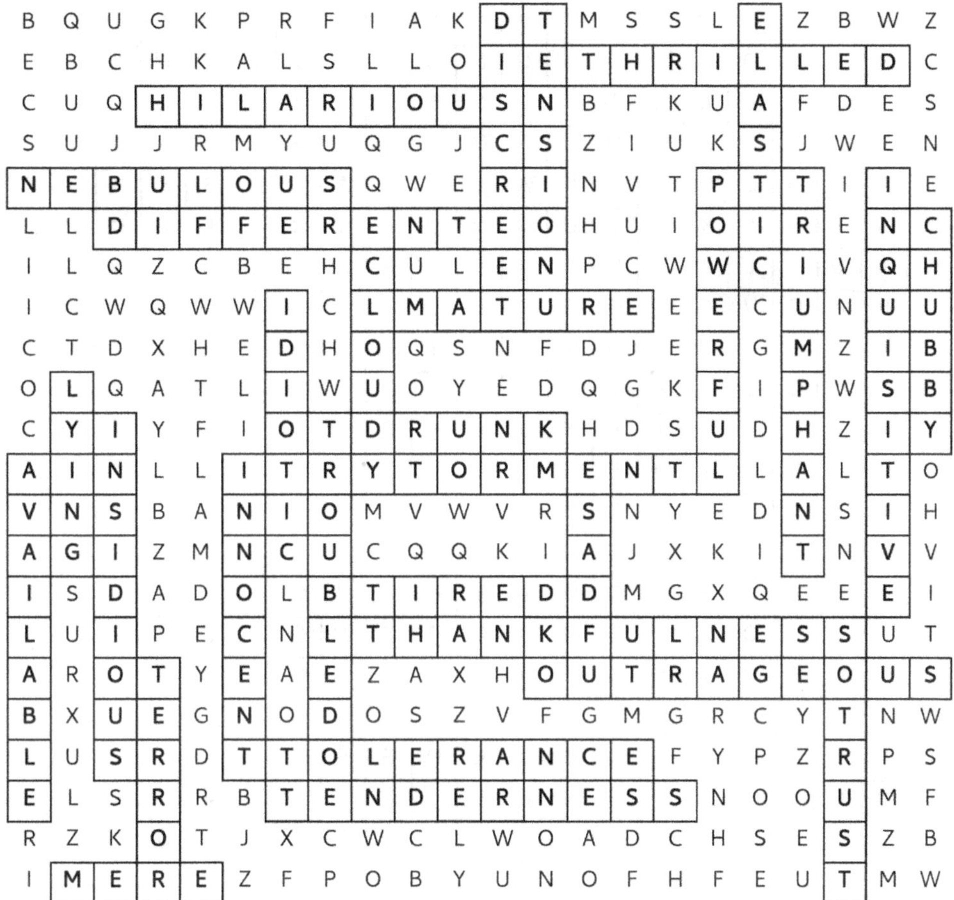

SOLUTIONS

10

MERE, ELASTIC, TIRED, NEBULOUS, INNOCENT, TROUBLED, TRUST, DRUNK, THANKFULNESS, TOLERANCE, THRILLED, CHUBBY, HILARIOUS, INQUISITIVE, CLOUDY, DISCREET, AVAILABLE, TERROR, INSIDIOUS, TENDERNESS, TRIUMPHANT, POWERFUL, IDIOTIC, TORMENT, OUTRAGEOUS, DIFFERENT, TENSION, LYING, MATURE, SAD

word search

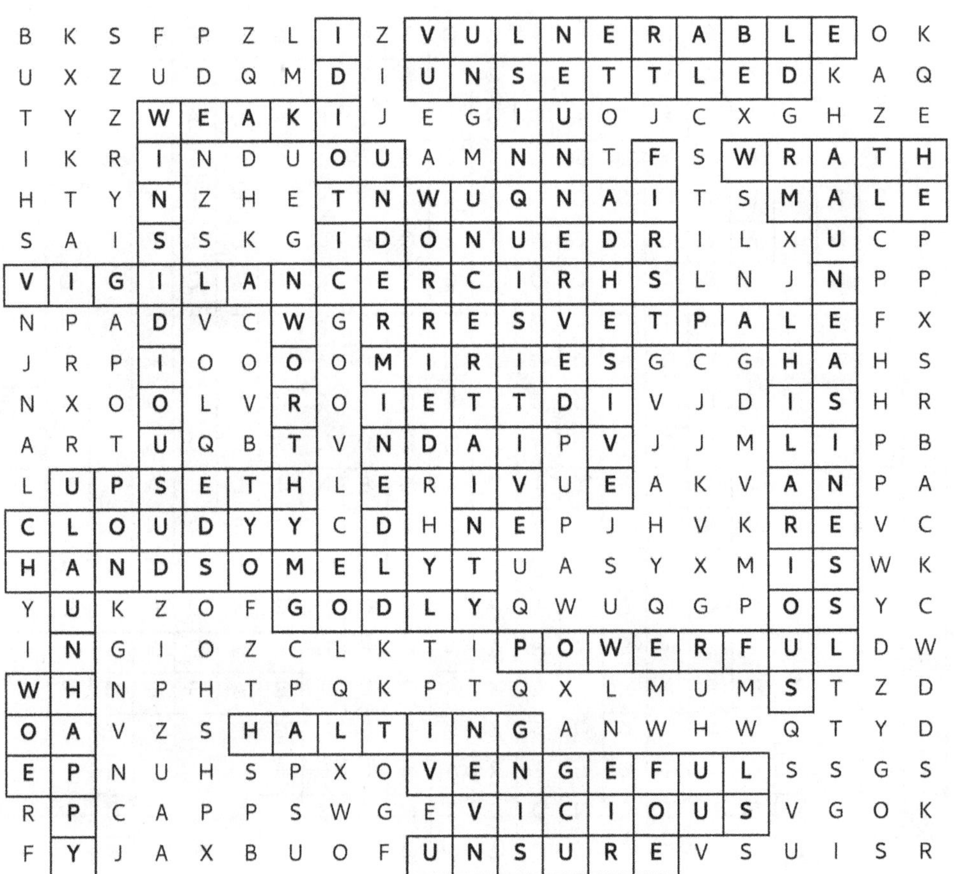

SOLUTIONS

11

ADHESIVE, VIGILANCE, HALTING, GODLY, UNCERTAINTY, POWERFUL, UNDERMINED, VICIOUS, IDIOTIC, WOE, HILARIOUS, WORTHY, PALE, UNEASINESS, CLOUDY, UNSURE, HANDSOMELY, UNSETTLED, FIRST, UNNERVED, WEAK, INSIDIOUS, VENGEFUL, WRATH, WORRIED, UNHAPPY, MALE, UPSET, INQUISITIVE, VULNERABLE

word search

www.ingramcontent.com/pod-product-compliance
Lightning Source LLC
Chambersburg PA
CBHW052111020426
42335CB00021B/2720

* 9 7 9 8 9 8 7 1 5 8 5 0 0 *